The Chronicle by
VENERABLE MOTHER MARY THERESA
nee
JOSEPHINE DUDZIK
1860 -1918

Documented and Pubished by
Rev. Henry Maria Malak - 1968

Updated by
Sr. Jeanne Marie Toriskie, OSF, PhD - 2020

- Handwritten manuscript in Polish by the author, Mother Mary Theresa Dudzik, in 1910
- Typed from the handwritten Chronicle and documented in Polish by Reverend Henry Malak in 1968
- Translated into English by Mary Hugoline Czaplinski, OSF; Beth Przeniczy, M.D. et alii in 1969
- Updated by Jeanne Marie Toriskie, OSF, Ph.D. in 2020

Copyright © 2020 by the Franciscan Sisters of Chicago. All rights reserved. This book or any portion thereof may not be reproduced or used in any manner whatsoever without the express written permission of the publisher except for the use of brief quotations in a book review.
Printed in the United States of America

First Printing, 1968
Second Printing, 2020

ISBN 978-1-7346179-1-7

Franciscan Sisters of Chicago
11500 Theresa Drive
Lemont, IL 60439

www.chicagofranciscans.com

TABLE OF CONTENTS

Historical Data from the Life of Mother Mary Theresa Dudzik vii
Historical Data from the Life of Josephine in the United States xi
    Historical Background xi
    Parochial Environment of St. Stanislaus Kostka Parish in Chicago xiv
    Josephine Dudzik xvi
Prologue xxi

The Chronicle or an Account of the Beginning of Our Community 1

First Thoughts and Plans, Aims and Objectives of Its Foundation Year 1893 3
    The Stirring of Religious Vocation 3
    Josephine Suggests the Founding of a Charitable Organization 3
    Year of Impatient Waiting 5

Year 1894 5
    First Co-Workers 5
    Founding a New Community 6
    Josephine and Mother Share Home with a Group 7
    Josephine's Promise 7
    December 8, 1894, Founding Date of New Community 8
    Permission Granted By Archbishop of Chicago 9
    Franciscanism — "We Were All Franciscan Tertiaries" 9
    Selection of Josephine as First Superior 9

Year 1895 10
    First Fruits of Community Life 11
    First Conflicts 11
    Conflicts Continued 12
    Heroic Readiness of the Foundress for Sacrifice 13

For Nine Years Sent to Work in Laundry 14
"With Lilting Soul" 15
The Matter of the Polish National Church 16
"This Religious Order Will Amount to Nothing" 16
"And I was Left Alone with Sister Angeline, Sister Josepha, and My Mother ... We Took a Smaller Apartment" 17
Further Difficulties 18
"I Had No Consolation Whatsoever" 19
Purchase of Land in Avondale 19
A Dispute with a Priest Over Payment 21
Painful Experience 21
Building Committee and "Welfare Society" 22
Foundress Goes Collecting 23
Humbling Self for the Good of the Cause 24
Matter of Building Home, Financial Problems 25
Foundress' Holy Obstinacy to Achieve Her Goal 26
Second Home — House Near St. Stanislaus Kostka Church 27

Year 1897 27

Flow of Elderly ... Joey, Legless Orphan 27
Not Just Material Aid, but Especially Spiritual Aid 28
Indifference of Committee 28
"St. Joseph, Our Manager" ... No Money in the Cashbox 29
"I Reminded Father Barzynski of the Necessity to Build" 30
Matchmaking the Foundress 31
"Everything Conspired Against Me" 32
Josephine, Superior of Rosary Confraternity, Co-Foundress of Arch-Confraternity of the Immaculate Heart of Mary 33
"Nothing Left For Building" 33
Construction of St. Joseph's Home Begins 34
Foundress Prays on Rising of St. Joseph Home 35
Mother Anne, Her Parents, and Sister Live in Avondale 35

Year 1898 36
New Vocations — Sisters Clara and Elizabeth 37
Farewell to St. Stanislaus Kostka, Move to Avondale 38
Difficulties in Supporting the Elderly and Crippled 38
Foundress in the Role of Carpenter 39
Dedication of St. Joseph Home 40
First Mass in the First Home Owned by Community 40
Management Problems — "How to Feed This Crowd" 41
Dismissal of Foundress from Office — Oct. 4, 1898 43
Reverend Andrew Spetz Steps into Life of New Community 44
"It Was My Favorite Holyday" 44
First Postulancy in the New Community 45
First Christmas in New Home ... No Organ 45
Conflicts that Led to the Dismissal of Foundress 47
Accusation Before Father Barzynski 48
Beginning of the Night of the Soul for Foundress 49

Year 1899 50
Father Barzynski Visits the Sisters for the Last Time 50
Father Barzynski is Hospitalized 51
Death of Spiritual Director 52
"The Greatest Grief Experienced in My Life" 52
"My Confessor Guided Me" 53
Heroic Submission to Divine Providence 53
Funeral of Father Barzynski — "What Will These Old Maids
  Do Now?" 53
"Providence Sent Us Another Father" 54
Confirmation of Community, Constitution, and Opening
  Novitiate 55
Blessed Sacrament in Tabernacle — First Time 55
Our Lady of Victory Statue 56
Foundress Begins Novitiate 56
Accepting a Crowd of Orphans 58

    Joey, Legless Orphan 58
    Construction of St. Vincent Orphanage and New Chapel 60

Year 1900: Jubilee Year 61
    Foundress (Novice) Burdened with Innumerable Duties 61
    First Vows in the Community — June 3, 1900 62
    Mother Becomes Novice Mistress 63
    Spiritual Sufferings of Mother Foundress 63
    Spiritual Training of Sisters 64

Year 1901 65
    First Renewal of Vows 66
    First Acceptance of Parochial School 66
    Office of the Blessed Virgin Mary 67

Year 1902 68
    Second Acceptance of Parochial School 68

Year 1903 69
    Purchase of Two Small Houses and Five Lots in Avondale 69
    Influx of Vocations 69
    Providential Mystery Gift 70
    Acceptance of Third Parochial School 70
    First 40 Hour Devotions in Community Chapel 70
    Portiuncula Indulgence for Community Chapel 71

Year 1904 71
    First Convent Infirmary 71
    Mother Anne's Illness 71
    First Visit of Archbishop of Chicago 72
    Blessed Kunegunda as Patroness of Community 72
    Embrace St. Elizabeth Nursery 73
    Fourth Parochial School Accepted 73
    Death of Agnes Dudzik, Mother of Mother Theresa 74

Year 1905 75
New House, Novitiate, and Laundry 75
New Laundry Upgraded 75
Archbishop Simon, Papal Delegate of Piux X 75
First Vocations from Cleveland, OH 76
Fifth and Sixth Schools Accepted by Community 77
Change of Superiors 78
Mother M. Theresa, Assistant 78
Sister M. Antonina, First Nurse in Community 78

Year 1906 79
Building of Historic Greenhouse 79
Twenty-Nine Novices 79
Seventh School Accepted 80
First Serious Illness of Mother Theresa 80

Year 1907 81
Mother Undergoes Surgery 81
Eighth School Accepted 81
Mother Theresa's Second Surgery 82
Statue of Blessed Kunegunda 82

Year 1908 82
Bishop's Visit — Confirmations 83
First Daily Mass Offered in Chapel 83
Death of First Sister in Community 84
Ninth School Accepted 84

Year 1909 85
Mother Theresa General Superior of Community 85
Spiritual Renewal of the Community 85
Father Andrew's Silver Jubilee of Priesthood 86
Father Andrew's Illness and His Return to Europe Thwarted
  Plans for Reform 86
Postponement of First General Chapter to 1910 87

Tenth and Eleventh Schools Accepted 88
Death of Elderly Chaplain 88
Mother Theresa's Perpetual Vows 89

Year 1910 90
"I Began Preparations for the First Chapter" 90
Twelfth School Accepted 90
Recollections for Sister Delegates to the First Chapter 91

Conclusion of Manuscript 92

Annotations 94

Epilogue 96

Appendix A — A Prayer for Our Daily Needs 104

Appendix B — Beatification Prayer for the Venerable Mother Mary Theresa Dudzik 105

Appendix C — Novena Prayer Through the Intercession of the Venerable Mother Mary Theresa Dudzik 106

Appendix D — How St. Francis Asked For and Obtained the Indulgence of Forgiveness 107

Appendix E — Chronological List of Quotations from Venerable Mother Mary Theresa Dudzik 109

Appendix F — List of Illustrations 114

Index 126

HISTORICAL DATA FROM THE LIFE OF MOTHER MARY THERESA DUDZIK

August 30, 1860	Birthday of Josephine Dudzik, later Mother Mary Theresa, in the village of Plocicz, in an urban parish of Kamien, Krajenski in Pomerania, Poland during its dismemberment by three partitioning powers.
September 2, 1860	Josephine's baptism in the parish church of Kamien, Krajenski.
1867 - 1875	Josephine attends school in Plocicz.
1872	Rose, Josephine's oldest sister, leaves for the United States and settles in Chicago.
1873 - 1874	Most probably the date of Josephine's First Holy Communion. All endeavors to obtain the document of that fact, in the parish as well as in the Bishop's Curia, were to no avail, as the archives were destroyed completely during the Second World War, 1939-1945.
1873	Maryann, the second oldest daughter of the Dudzik family, comes to Chicago.

1876 - 1880	Period of Josephine's schooling in tailoring in Kamien Krajenski.
1878	Maryann dies in Chicago. Her orphaned daughter, Anna, was adopted by Rose who already had 13 children of her own.
1880	Frances, the fifth child in the family, follows Maryann to Chicago. (Later she enters the Order of the Sisters of Notre Dame, where she dies as Sister Mary Leowina.)
May 1881 (?)	Josephine[1], her parents, and the rest of the family come to Chicago and settle in the only Polish parish at that time, St. Stanislaus Kostka Parish.

---

1 Explanatory Note: From her arrival here, Josephine, a well-trained and qualified tailoress makes herself independent. Unlike other immigrant young ladies who worked in a factory or did housework, she operated her own tailor shop. Historical sources show as follows: She has very many wealthy clients, her income is high and she is the sole support of her parents.

December 8, 1883	Frances, the younger sister of Josephine, enters the Community of the Sisters of Notre Dame in Milwaukee, WI.
June 6, 1884	Catherine, the youngest sister, enters the Sisters of the Incarnate Word Order, in San Antonio, TX.
November 28, 1886	The 18-year old Catherine, Sister M. Barbara, a nurse, dies in Texas in an accident while returning to the convent from a sick patient.
May 12, 1889	John Dudzik, the father of Mother Theresa, dies at the age of 66. The chronicles of St. Stanislaus Kostka Parish, Chicago, state that he was buried the very same day in St. Adalbert Cemetery. The cause of his death is not given. It is left to us to solve the question - why the immediate burial? Was it because of some epidemic, which was prevalent in Chicago at that time?
October 24, 1904	After the father's death, only Mother Theresa[2] and her 60-year-old mother are left in the family residence. Mother Theresa's mother died October 24, 1904, in the first home for the aged, founded[3] by her daughter.

---

[2] Private Acts of Mercy: but, simultaneously (and again we base our statements on historical sources), she performs public acts of charity and even plans how to organize this work as a social project. As the first step, she influences other young ladies to find interest in it. Confirmation of this fact is found on the very first page of her manuscript, and in this case of this typewritten copy.

[3] So much for the most important data pertaining to the personage of Mother Mary Theresa until her entrance on the way of founding a new community, whose chronicled deeds will be unwound for the reader on the pages of this compilation.

x

HISTORICAL DATA FROM THE LIFE OF JOSEPHINE IN THE UNITED STATES

HISTORICAL BACKGROUND

It will be difficult for the reader of Mother Mary Theresa to get the feel of her times and her "reasons" for establishing a new Religious Community, without at least a superficial knowledge of the historical background of that period.

They are years of social ferment, which rolls over the North American continent in waves. Besides the native social phenomena, peculiar solely to this terrain, the youthful United States are not entirely free of the influence of the European brand of social unrest, reaching across the ocean. Socialism and Communism, celebrating the triumphs in Europe, reach boldly across the ocean and sink their roots in the new soil. Anarchy in particular, throttled in Europe by the totalitarian governments of the emperors, czars, and kings, is unhampered in its activities on the free soil.

The Haymarket Riot in Chicago in May 1886.

The bomb thrown in Chicago in May of 1886, which killed several policemen and wounded many others, and the sentencing to death of the assassins is only one of the many episodes of that period. The cry of the condemned man from the gallows, "Long live anarchy," was an expression of the temperament of the working masses of that time in their battle with capitalistic exploitation. At that time, the exploited laborer had no legal weapons to defend himself against the greed of the industrial potentates.

Perhaps the most authoritative illustration of the times and the situation of the laboring masses are the words of President Theodore

Roosevelt, quoted from his autobiography[4], "... These are," he writes about the housing conditions of the laboring class, "one-room residences, where cigars are manufactured day and night without ceasing. In the same compartment where men are working, women and children eat, sleep and live. I was told that in one room there lived a large family and a tenant. Here actually lived and worked three men, two women and many children. Tobacco was heaped up everywhere, even on the sleeping litters and in the corner where portions of discarded food lay. The  inhabitants worked until late at night, in the same room where they ate and slept...." In such conditions, living masses of the municipal proletariat were smitten again and again by waves of economic depression, when there was lack of work even in this tobacco industry, in the overcrowded stuffy rooms.

In general, all historians and sociologists investigating those times assume that the most characteristic cross-section of conditions in the juvenile United States was Chicago. It was then considered the Queen of the Great Lakes. It was situated on the great continental crossroads running  from East to West and from North to South. Already Chicago was the greatest grain and meat trade center in the world; therefore, it was affected much more by the waves of social turmoil, strikes, and revolutions. "On the boundary line of civilization," writes a

---

4 p. 89 -90.

historian of 1890, "a powerful city was being formed — a metropolis of the Middle West, opened especially to immigrant masses flocking there from the four winds. Chicago at this time is the most characteristic melting pot of different nationalities and races, among whom native-born Americans constituted only a small percent."

To throw some light on the diverse population at that time, it will suffice to quote only a few statistics from 1890:

Germans	384,958	Native Americans	292,463
Irish	215,536	Polish	52,756

The rest of the inhabitants in the city with a population of over one million two hundred thousand, distributed themselves among 30 different nationalities with immigrants predominating.

A tremendous exhibit takes place in Chicago in 1893, on the occasion of the four hundredth anniversary of the discovery of America by Columbus. Preparation for it and the exhibit year itself provides employment for the laborer. The city and its inhabitants experience moments of relative abundance. But the closing of this enterprise rebounds so much more tragically on the city as a whole. We now witness thousands of unemployed, an oncoming severe winter, the growing number of the destitute, a heavy wave of renewed strikes, among which the Pullman strike becomes the symptom of a most  painful calamity, and finally the assassination of President Harrison. All of the above throw sufficient light on the historical background of the city, in which the young Josephine Dudzik, the future Mother Theresa, begins her work of mercy.

History of those days throws the following light on the social conditions of Chicago: "Economic Crisis of 1893"[5] "... led to a great railroad strike and to labor riots of dimensions thus far unknown in America, which President Cleveland endeavored to stifle with the help of the federal army."

The young maiden, Josephine Dudzik, "declares war on these lamentable conditions in her own way"... Which? How? We will find the answer on the very first page of her present manuscript.

PAROCHIAL ENVIRONMENT OF ST. STANISLAUS KOSTKA PARISH IN CHICAGO

As is evident from the statistics, the Polish people numbered over fifty-two thousand out of the one million two hundred thousand inhabitants in Chicago in 1890. This fosters an observation that many Poles, depending on the partition from which they migrated, were drawn under a nationality, be it German, Austrian or Russian. Today, it is difficult to establish the exact number. However, taking into consideration the fact that in 1890 there were eight Polish parishes in Chicago, we assume that the number of Poles, in all certainty, must have been greater than the statistics given.

But this is not our concern at present. In connection with Mother Theresa and her work, we are interested in Chicago's oldest Polish parish, St. Stanislaus Kostka, organized in 1867. Its boundary extended a few miles from the center of Chicago, near the Chicago River, in the vicinity of field crossroads known today as: Noble and Bradley Streets. Chroniclers of 1867 and those of later years add an interesting detail, that about this parochial grouping, were stretched waste lands where meeting an Indian or having a wild beast approach the buildings was not at all rare.

---

5 From Mother's manuscript we learn that exactly then, in 1893, she makes her first proposal to organize active works of mercy.

When the Dudzik family arrived in Chicago in 1881 and settled in that parish, the conditions had changed considerably. The parish, strengthened with a flow of Polish immigrants, grows to an extraordinary size, and when in 1890, Josephine Dudzik begins her private works of mercy, the parish is a colossus equal to many dioceses in Italy.

St. Stanislaus Kostka Parish in Chicago gives the following statistical data from 1893:

Baptisms	2,277
Marriages	382
Funerals	883

About 4,000 children in the parochial school were divided into 50 classes. The school was under the direction of 60 Sisters of Notre Dame, who were commissioned by the Resurrectionist Fathers.[6] This school was considered to be the largest Catholic school in the United States.[7]

In 1893, there were 45 organizations, both religious and fraternal in the parish, comprising a commonwealth of about 12,000 members. The parish choir numbered approximately 300 members. This necessitated a division into several groups. The confraternity of the Holy Rosary having 4,500 members was also divided into separate groups.

In addition, there was St. Stanislaus Kostka College staffed by the priests, and an active dramatic club and an auditorium with a seating capacity

---

6 *Golden Jubilee Memoir*, p. 25.
7 Parenthetically, we add, in order to underline the above, that when in 1906 the school had burned down with the indispensable archives of the parish organizations, and a new school was erected, the Vice President of the United States came to the dedication and Archbishop Quigley officiated in the presence of a great number of clergy.

of 6,000. Here the renowned artist, Helen Modrzejewska, frequently entertained with her amusing performances. At that time this hall was known as the most spacious in the city of Chicago, so besides the local performances, Polish National Congresses and assemblies were also held here.

There also existed in the parish: an orphanage accommodating almost one hundred children, four libraries, a daily newspaper, THE CHICAGO DAILY, with its publication and a whole series of lesser....

How many members were there in the parish at that time? It is difficult to give the exact number. From the Fathers' letters petitioning help from their Motherhouse in Rome, we learn that during the Easter time several thousand penitents were awaiting them by the confessionals. And from the ciphers given above referring to the organizations, we permit ourselves to assume the number to be between 30 to 40 thousand souls. Some authors do not hesitate to accept the number of 50 thousand souls.

One thing is sure, that the parish is "a huge mill" as one of the Resurrectionists describes it, in his letter to the authorities, "a mill crushing the few priests" who at that time labored in the parish.

JOSEPHINE DUDZIK

And so, in the above sketched historical background, as well as in the rapidly advancing life of the oldest Polish parish in the city dwells a young maiden, Josephine Dudzik. She herself as Mother Mary Theresa, in holy obedience to her spiritual director, sketches the present "Chronicle." She writes, "and I was well-known in the entire parish, serving the church for 16 years ...."

These words are written by a Mother whose outstanding trait is the heroic virtue of humility. No, Mother had not written too much. On the contrary, in this sentence is contained her admirable humility. Toilsome research in St. Stanislaus Kostka Parish's chronicled notations, partly published in print, indicate to what extent Mother, as a young lady had taken active participation in the life of that colossal parish.

From 1885 to 1898, Josephine is a superior of the Young Ladies Rosary Confraternity, Group II. Several hundred members belong to this group. At about the same time, until 1898 she is the superior of the Arch-confraternity of the Immaculate Heart of Mary, from which (as the Chronicles state) "over a hundred were eventually married, and about forty young ladies entered the Religious life." From 1886, that is, from the time it was

canonically erected, Josephine is chosen the mistress of novices in the Third Order and remains in office until 1898.

The reader may be startled that Mother, in spite of the founding of the Congregation in 1894, still holds the office in the above-mentioned societies until 1898. The explanation is that until 1898, Mother and her very young Community are still in St. Stanislaus Kostka Parish, and only when in March of the same year she transfers the clustering group with herself to Avondale, that she resigns from the mentioned positions. The young maiden, who from among a thousand of equals in the parish, was selected to the above offices, must have had uncommon leadership values, which qualified her for these positions. Yet, the three above-mentioned offices are only those which the writer had confirmed on the basis of chronicled sources. Josephine's participation in organizations in the parish was probably much more than can be accounted for at present. Care of altars, vestments and church linens, participation in choir, does not all that entitle one to say, "I was well-known in the parish"?

And yet we have left out another extremely important segment of Josephine's participation in parish life, which was to have bearing on her entire future, namely her apostolate of mercy, in which the pastor of this parish, Reverend Vincent Barzynski, C.R., considers her as his right hand.

To make this segment clearer to the reader, let us present but a few facts from the turning point of 1890 to 1894, that is, until the moment of the founding of the Congregation.

Just a glance at the *Dziennik Chicagoski* annals of the years mentioned, will lead one to a profound understanding to what catastrophical depth were the waves of economical failures imbedded in the St. Stanislaus Kostka parochial immigrant society who were branded as a lower social group. What characteristic light is being cast on this group from the *Dziennik Chicagoski* press, which repeatedly exhorted

them to "emigrate" from the city to the western rural states to the mines or to forestry. And again this "emigration" of the Chicago immigrants is recorded and confirmed in history. Obviously, it was not the older element, but the healthiest of the youth who summoned up the courage to seek these new "adventures." Misery, unemployment and hunger are proverbially ill counsellors. In many cases these young "emigrants" left their aged, disabled and infirm parents to the mercy of fate.... In addition, an exceptionally severe winter was approaching. The Chicago newspapers (not only Polish) were filled with desperate calls for aid for the great masses of the homeless. The situation was so desperately miserable that the city mayor was forced to open the fire stations, the railway stations, libraries and even City Hall to give shelter to the needy.

The Pastor of St. Stanislaus Kostka Parish, after exhausting all possibilities, gave both church vestibules for overnight lodging. Only on this background the reader will be able to understand what Mother writes on the very first page of her manuscript: ... "I had them (poor homeless, frequently too many, in my home because of lack of space ... but when Father Vincent (Reverend Vincent Barzynski, the Pastor) had any problem with a poor woman, he himself came with her or sent her to me to get care. I could not refuse, because I felt their misery and suffering."

And then during the oncoming severe winter of 1893,[8] Josephine, for the first time, presents her plan for organizing a group of young ladies, who would be willing to make sacrifices in order to help the unfortunate.

---

8 According to the National Weather Service, the Chicago winter of 1893 calculated from December 1892 to March 1893 averaged 22.5° F, a tie with the winter of 1977-78. These were the third coldest Chicago winters in the history of weather records. The second coldest Chicago winter averaged 22.3°F in 1903-4, also during Mother Theresa's lifetime. The coldest Chicago winter occurred in 2013-14 and averaged 22°F.

PROLOGUE

One of the requirements of Canon Law concerning preparatory acts to the canonization of an individual is an obligation to publish her various writings. Since the congregation of the Franciscan Sisters of Blessed Kunegunda[9] commissioned the preparation of this document of the foundress of their Community, Mother Mary Theresa Dudzik, to the undersigned, at the request of Mother Mary Beatrice and Council, I am presenting in typewritten form a collection of her writings. The original manuscript of the same is kept in the archives of the Community at the General Motherhouse. The present chronicle is a true copy of the original[10], containing the exact number of pages as well as various blunders or orthographical mistakes.

Since the chronicle was written over 50 years ago and refers to many places, events, and people totally unfamiliar today, it seems necessary to footnote the chronicle with clarifying explanations. These footnotes are not intended to interpret the events recounted by Mother Theresa, but to explain their significance. Therefore, any implied interpretation found in the footnotes is unintentional. As is customary, numerical references are found in the right margin; documentation is at the bottom of the page.

To all those who would be interested in a much greater, fundamental study of the life of Mother, I would recommend as an extensive "Commentary" to her present writings, an officially published biography under the title of, *The Apostle of Mercy from Chicago*[11]. It may be acquired at the Central Office of the League

---

9 In 1970, the Franciscan Sisters of Blessed Kunegunda changed their name to the Franciscan Sisters of Chicago.
10 This current edition of 2019 does not follow the original pagination, and includes illustrations, photos, updated historical information and graphic elements to highlight the reader's experience of the life of Venerable Mother Mary Theresa Dudzik.
11 The biography is out of print.

of Mother Mary Theresa in Lemont, IL, 1220 Main Street[12]. A division of "Annotations" is found at the end of the script for further explanation.

Reverend Henry Maria Malak,[13]
Postulator

---

[12] Information about the life and Cause of Venerable Mary Theresa Dudzik may now be obtained from the Franciscan Sisters of Chicago, 11400 Theresa Drive, Lemont IL 60439.

[13] "Born on All Saints' Day, November 1, 1912, in the village of Sadki, Poland, Father Malak ... became interested in the life of Josephine Dudzik, later Mother Mary Theresa of the Franciscan Sisters of Chicago (founded December 8, 1894). He wrote a biography of their founder in 1962 and began publishing a periodical bulletin entitled "The Apostle of Mercy from Chicago." In 1963 he was appointed to Lemont, IL, and until 1972 he was Postulator in the Archdiocese of Chicago for her beatification. During the remaining years of his life, he continued his labors for the cause of Mother Mary Theresa, completing a fuller version of her biography and establishing a museum of her personal effects in Lemont. Following his death on June 19, 1987, he was buried in Lemont, not far from the grave of Mother Mary Theresa." http://www.amazon.com/Henry-M.-Malak/e/B00CAW1DAW

THE CHRONICLE

or

An Account of the Beginning of Our Community

First Thoughts and Plans, Aims and Objectives of Its Foundation Year 1893

The stirring of religious vocation

For a number of years I had already been contemplating in what way better comfort and lodging could be given to poor girls, widows, and to the sick who were unable to do hard work. I had frequently sheltered too many of them in the limited quarters of my home. As a result, my mother often hindered[14] me in my work of mercy because she was exposed to various inconveniences, for which I was reproached. She also remarked that not only I suffered, but that this action of mine compelled her to suffer, too.

Josephine suggests the founding of a charitable organization

I would then make promises that I would not accept any more of the poor. Nevertheless, as soon as Father Vincent[15] had any trouble with such an unfortunate one, he would either escort her or send her to me to be taken care of. I could not refuse to comply with his wishes since I felt the misery and sufferings of others; and it seemed to me that I could not love Jesus, or even expect

> *I felt the misery and sufferings of others; and it seemed to me that I could not love Jesus, or even expect heaven, if I were concerned only about myself and my mother—not to suffer any inconvenience, but simply to live in comfort.*

---

14 "hindered". Directed by sane judgment and prudence, she tried to subdue her daughter in her "raging" enthusiasm of mercy, taking into account the housing shortages in the small bungalow. The same mother later became a silent co-worker of her daughter.
15 "Father Vincent". Reverend Vincent Barzynski, C.R. was an envoy delegated from Rome in 1866 to Santa Maria, TX. In 1874 he became a pastor of the largest Polish parish in Chicago, St. Stanislaus Kostka, where he remained until his death in 1899.

heaven, if I were concerned only about myself and my mother, not to suffer any inconvenience, but simply to live in comfort.

Very often I felt a persistent urge to make greater sacrifices for others. Consequently, I was especially guided with a continuous thought of how I could be of service to the needy and the poor. In my mind, I was already arranging the beds and preparing all things necessary for this purpose. This thought haunted me day and night, even though I was unaware of the means by which this could be accomplished. While at prayer, a thought suddenly occurred to me to rent or purchase a house in the vicinity of St. Stanislaus Kostka Church and assemble all the tertiaries from this parish, who would desire to lead a life in common and to pray and work to support this project. I also thought of some pious young ladies whom I knew, especially those who were formerly in a convent, such as the one who was a Felician Sister for twelve years; and I felt that they could teach me much that I did not know, including the art of prayer and union with God.

Consoled somewhat by this thought, I decided to confide in my sodalist friend, Rose Wisinski, who usually advised me concerning the problems and difficulties in the Rosary Society. She[16] praised this plan and expressed her willingness to join us; but her parents and an invalid sister were an immediate impediment.[17] I tried to console Rose and suggested that she might be able to take her parents along with her. We made plans to discuss this issue at the next meeting with the young ladies of the Third Order of St. Francis.

---

16 Rose Wisinski entered the new Community under the name of Sister Anna. In 1898 she was appointed a Superior by Reverend Barzynski. She was the first Mother General from 1910 to 1916. The young Sisters thought that she was the foundress of the Community.

17 The parents, as well as the crippled sister of Sister Anna, later lived with her in the first Motherhouse.

Year of impatient waiting

The regular monthly meeting of the Third Order of St. Francis was held on Sunday, October 1, 1893. After transacting the business of the meeting, I presented our plans to the assembled tertiaries. The members accepted the proposition joyfully and some, including myself, requested its immediate fulfillment. Rose Wisinski, nevertheless, advised the group that she considered it more appropriate to pray for one year for the intention of recognizing God's Will; I readily consented, although a year seemed to be so very long.

Year 1894

After the year elapsed, the meeting was again held on the feast of Our Lady of the Rosary, that is, on October 7, 1894. I reminded the tertiaries about the resolutions made a year ago and inquired about the promised prayers. I discovered that some had completely forgotten the issue, while others, overjoyed by this reminder, wanted to join the group. Consequently, I made the following decision: all those who wished to join were asked to submit their names—only Rose Wisinski was unable to enlist presently because of her parents and mute sister. Therefore, seven members, who had no parents or permanent lodging, applied for admission; I was the eighth one.

First Co-Workers

The names of the eight volunteers were as follows: Josephine Dudzik, Mary B., Mary S., Catherine M., Susanne C., Clara S., Victoria M., and Rose Wisinski.

I then informed the volunteers that this whole matter would be presented to our spiritual Father, the Reverend Vincent Barzynski, and I would seek his advice on how to proceed in this regard.[18]

Lacking both straightforwardness and the necessary courage to approach Father Barzynski immediately, I waited with this proposition until November 2; I then took advantage of the opportunity to inform him about our plans. They were received very favorably. Father said that we were not allowed to oppose a good cause, but we should promote it and help in bringing it to a successful fruition. In turn, he promised to aid us with his counsel.

> *Father said that we were not allowed to oppose a good cause, but we should promote it and help in bringing it to a successful fruition.*

Founding a new Community

There was one thing which Father said, however, that struck my attention and somewhat frightened me. He would not sanction the project unless we lived under religious obedience and wore the religious garb. I decided to overcome this fear and to obey him in everything that he might command in this respect.

Father then told me to ask those who had submitted their names to assemble together on November 10. They would be interviewed by him personally and privately; and each one's possessions, which were to be transferred into the common treasury, would be recorded. At this meeting, our general aim of helping poor girls, widows, and sick women was changed at a suggestion from Father to another aim. We were now to care for aged and disabled persons, but not in a home on Noble Street near St. Stanislaus Kostka Church, but in Avondale or Cragin. All agreed and accepted Father's decision, with the exception of Susanne C., who was disappointed and unhappy at the thought of leaving Chicago. She was also unwilling to part with the thousand dollars that she possessed and had to hand it in to the common fund upon joining the group.

---

18 In view of this, some authors claimed Reverend Barzynski as founder of the Community.

Josephine and mother share home with a group

At the second meeting which convened on Sunday, November 24, 1894, Father Barzynski suggested that we all move into one home. The candidate who had the largest living quarters was to accept the group into her home. Here we were to pass a six-month probation period, after which we were to receive our habits. I was a little astounded upon hearing this and wondered how we could walk around in a religious garb and move from one temporary residence to another. It then occurred to me that St. Francis had no permanent quarters either; and this thought brought me peace of mind. The building finally designated as our first residence, was my home on 11 Chapin Street.

> *It then occurred to me that St. Francis had no permanent quarters either; and this thought brought me peace of mind.*

At this very same meeting, held on November 24, Constance Topolinski, hearing about our plans, joined the group and was accepted by Father Barzynski. He told us to begin a novena to the Immaculate Conception of the Blessed Virgin Mary on the 27th of November, jointly with the parishioners in church. Since the novena was to be offered in our intention, we began it with the greatest devotion and begged the Mother of God for help in this difficult undertaking which now confronted us.

> *Since the novena was to be offered in our intention, we began it with the greatest devotion and begged the Mother of God for help in this difficult undertaking which now confronted us.*

Josephine's Promise

Our last joint meeting took place on December 12, but I had a few more private interviews with Father Vincent. He examined and tried me in various ways, but it seemed to me that with the help of God I would be capable of accomplishing everything. He also demanded a promise from me that I would care for this Community not only in its time of prosperity but also in times of trouble, and when difficulties would beset it from all sides. Actually at this moment, I did not foresee any problems and thought that everything would go smoothly.

Reverend Barzynski was a saintly man, and he foretold the great difficulties and adversities that I would have to face. He had explained it all to me so plainly that I was fully aware of my obligations when making that promise. This knowledge was most beneficial to me against my lack of serious judgment. When the prediction was beginning to materialize within a short span of time, I reflected on it and recalled my promise; consequently, I was able to bear it more easily. The thought that I deliberately agreed on this undertaking for Jesus Christ is still an incentive till this day for me, who am so full of self-love.

> He also demanded a promise from me that I would care for this Community not only in its time of prosperity but also in times of trouble and when difficulties would beset it from all sides.

> The thought that I deliberately agreed on this undertaking for Jesus Christ is still an incentive till this day for me....

December 8, 1894, founding date of new Community

At the joint meeting of the group, Father interviewed each of us separately and asked what was our desire, motive, and decision. He wrote down our answers. At this time Clara S., who intended to join another Community, left the group. Father then blessed us and said that we would already be together for Christmas. He also announced that the date for the beginning of our Community would be December 8, 1894, and that it would be dedicated under the patronage of the Immaculate Conception of the Mother of God.

Our Community, consequently, begins on the above-mentioned day and year.

Permission granted by Archbishop of Chicago

The Reverend Vincent Barzynski is rightfully considered as our first main founder,[19] we were established as a Community with the permission[20] of the diocesan Ordinary of that time, the Most Reverend Archbishop Feehan.

In accordance with Father Vincent's wishes expressed at the last meeting, all the members of the group came to my home. The last one to arrive on December 20 was Sister Mary Angelina.[21] When I notified Father about this, he told me that on the following Sunday, December 23, 1894, we should elect a Superior by means of drawing lots. He explained the procedure which we were to use, and I followed his instructions conscientiously. On the designated day, Rose Wisinski also came for the election. Although she was always united with us in spirit, she could not live with us because of her filial commitments to her aged and sick parents; she was eagerly waiting for the day when we would move into our own home.

Archbishop Patrick Augustine Feehan

Franciscanism — "We were all Franciscan tertiaries"

Besides me, the following were present at the election: Rose Wisinski, Mary B., Catherine M., Mary S., Victoria M., and Constance Topolinski. Everyone present was a tertiary.

Selection of Josephine as first Superior

After an invocation to the Holy Spirit and to the Mother of God, each one wrote the name of the one whom she wished to have as a Superior.

---

19 The reference to Father Barzynski as founder cannot be taken literally. It becomes understandable if one considers Father's relationship to Josephine as her confessor and spiritual director, and also speaks of Josephine's own humility.
20 The permission was orally given.
21 Sister Angelina was the last one to join the group. She died in the Community in 1930.

Six votes were cast for me, and in this manner I became the first Superior. I held that office from December 23, 1894, to October 4, 1898. After this election, we all changed our baptismal names to the ones we received at the Third Order Investiture and called ourselves as follows: Sister Theresa, Sister Anna, Sister Hyacinth, Sister Frances, Sister Felixa, Sister Joachim, and Sister Angelina.²²

On Christmas Eve we prepared the traditional supper and invited Father Barzynski, who had previously informed me that on that day he would bless our temporary quarters. He came as he had promised, approved the election, blessed the home, and broke the traditional Christmas wafer with us for the first and last time. After bestowing his blessing upon us, he promised to formulate a daily program of prayers and duties which we were to observe. We invited him for supper, but he refused since his duty was to be together with the priests at the rectory.

During the Christmas Eve supper, we were all very happy, especially I, for it seemed to me that I had already attained my goal and that the days would continue in joy. The other Sisters were, more or less, of the same spirit. The rest of the Christmas holydays was spent in the same free and happy atmosphere.

Year 1895

On the 15th of January, 1895, I received the daily program which Father Vincent had promised to write for us. His many duties kept him from completing this task sooner.²³

---

22 From this group, only Mother M. Theresa, Sister Anna, and Sister Angelina persevered.
23 During this period St. Stanislaus Kostka parish consisted of over thirty thousand souls. For this reason Father Barzynski was unable give the constant help which he would have liked to offer.

First fruits of community life

Beginning with that day, we performed our spiritual exercises in common — prayers, meditation, and spiritual reading. We had, however, no appropriate book for meditation. When Father Simon,[24] the Superior of the Resurrectionist Fathers at St. Stanislaus Kostka Rectory heard of this, he gave us an old book, *The Year of Christ*, which served us for our daily meditations for over thirteen years. Father Vincent donated *Spiritual Life*, which we used for spiritual reading before dinner. The order of the day was about the same, with only a few exceptions: rising in the morning was at 4:30; daily meditation time was fifteen minutes, with an additional five minutes during Lent. It was followed by the Litany to the Holy Name of Jesus, the Little Hours, and the regular Third Order prayers. We tried, as much as possible, to observe this order of the day, although some of us found it quite difficult to do so. We devoted the rest of the day to the following duties: sewing ladies' dresses; washing clothes at St. Stanislaus rectory, and likewise cleaning the rectory.

First conflicts

The long-cherished desire for the common life faded away in time. When we assembled together to lead a new life, we brought in all that we possessed and placed it in the treasury to be used as a common fund. One of us, however, Sister Joachim, would not accede to this regulation. She kept her trunk locked and gave rise to dissatisfaction and murmuring among the others to an ever-increasing degree. I felt that what she did was improper; I sent an order to Sister Joachim through another Sister, either to give up her possessions and have them placed in the common fund or to leave. She became angry at my giving the order through someone else instead of giving it to her directly; she left us on the 28th of January, 1895.

---

24 Reverend Simon Kobrzynski took an active part in the battling that occurred over Czarist Russia. He was appointed as an aide at St. Stanislaus Kostka parish in Chicago. This book, *The Year of Christ*, exists today in the Postulary quarters of Mother Mary Theresa's Cause.

Father Vincent was very disappointed with me and told me that it was my duty to take care of such problems personally. I, in turn, told Father that it was very difficult for me to give orders or to correct others.[25] Very seriously, Father then said that if I cannot tell anyone anything, it would be better if we were to disband at once and discontinue causing him any more trouble.

Conflicts continued

That statement worried and saddened me. Having resolved that I would rather deny myself than to disband, I apologized to Father and begged him to forgive me. It was my first act of self-denial for this cause, and it cost me very much. Father allowed us to continue and to prove ourselves. I was very happy on hearing this and thought that such incidents would never occur again. But my hopes were short-lived. In the early part of February I noticed signs of dissatisfaction again. As I have mentioned before, we were engaged in sewing and washing clothes, and everyone was assigned a definite task. Sister Angelina and I occupied ourselves with sewing since we were professional seamstresses; we had very much to do. Sister Frances, Sister Hyacinth, and Sister Felixa had been appointed for washing clothes at the rectory. Everyone had work suitable to her abilities, and all the money earned was to be saved for the new home. All went well from the beginning, but dissatisfaction slowly crept in. The three Sisters, engaged in washing clothes, felt that the work was too hard for them; they thought that the Superior and Sister Angelina just relaxed at home.

> *It was my first act of self-denial for this cause, and it cost me very much.*

> *Everyone had work suitable to her abilities....*

---

25 That characteristic feature of Mother M. Theresa soon shall become the cause of several sorrowful experiences. Being naturally gentle, she preferred that many an evil pass in silence.

Heroic readiness of the Foundress for sacrifice

One morning, on our way to church to hear Holy Mass, a quarrel began. I was stunned since I didn't suspect anything. Sister Frances remained at home and said nothing to me; I presumed that she was sick, without being aware that anger was her motive for not being with the group. Ordinarily, after returning home from Mass, we would continue our prayer and meditation, while my mother, who lived with us and was feeling quite well at the time, prepared breakfast with the help of Sister Felixa's mother who stayed with us. This enabled us to hear Mass, say our prayers, and meditate without leaving our places at prayer to begin preparing breakfast. Mother even prepared the other meals when she was up to par.

On this particular morning, however, Sister Frances stayed behind and complained about us to the mothers in derogatory terms. When we came in and began our prayers, we heard loud and angry bickering in the kitchen. I quickly went there and found both mothers almost on the verge of tears, disturbed and hurt by what they heard. Before I could pacify Sister and bring peace to the poor mothers, the time for meditation had passed. I came to the conclusion that I must go to wash clothes in order to set a good example[26] and to show that I never intended to shun hard work.

I had been ordered by the doctor to refrain from doing hard work and had obeyed his instructions for a few years. Yet, when it was necessary to sacrifice myself in order to bring peace, I did not hesitate; I went forth, trusting in the good God, and He came to my aid. I began my new work out; truthfully speaking, I felt sick at the beginning. However, with God's help I didn't have to stay in bed even for a day; I was able to cultivate such love for this task that I remained fulfilling it, without a break, for nine years. When I noticed that my health had not been a bit impaired by the heavy work, I strove to choose the hardest task. I note this,

> *Yet, when it was necessary to sacrifice myself in order to bring peace, I did not hesitate; I went forth, trusting in the good God, and He came to my aid.*

---

26   This is a characteristic feature of Mother M. Theresa. "Mother Theresa was first in two special circumstances," declares one of her former novices. "Always first in the most difficult work, and always first in the chapel."

not to praise myself, but to reveal God's evident assistance. My mother, realizing that I was doing such hard work, was saddened and often cried; she thought that I would die prematurely.

> *I strove to choose the hardest task. I note this, not to praise myself, but to reveal God's evident assistance.*

For nine years sent to work in laundry

It never occurred to me that I would die sooner because of the strenuous work that I was undertaking. Sister Hyacinth, the instigator of all that murmuring, friction, and misunderstanding, was now left at home to take my place in sewing, cooking, and washing our clothes. Soon, however, she grew tired of her new tasks and renewed her complaints that this work was too hard for her.

On the 2nd of April, Father Barzynski was informed of her intention of leaving the convent and returning to her mother. But she could find no peace of mind at home and begged me urgently to take her back. After repeated pleadings on her part, Father Vincent granted permission for her to be accepted. She returned on the 4th of April, the feast of Our Lady of Sorrows. She was not too happy since she now had to occupy the last place, whereas formerly, she ranked second, right after me. She cried often. Her dissatisfaction with the place, as well as with the work assigned her, was quite evident.

Another tertiary, Catherine G., also joined our group on April 4. She was now called Sister Josepha, after the name she received in the Third Order. Her attitude showed quite plainly that a life lived under religious obedience was not for her; consequently, she left the Community on August 14, 1898, after being with us for three years and five months. Although she was sickly, she was a most reliable and responsible worker; she had been my right hand in every task.[27]

---

[27] Mother wrote the above words in obedience to her confessor, Father Andrew Spetz, C.R., during the year 1895.

Easter was soon approaching. We shared the traditional Easter egg with one another, but not with the exuberant joy that we had experienced at Christmas time when we shared the wafer. There was one in the group who continually cried for some reason. I was of a happy disposition, and I never liked crying of any kind. Although I hummed "Haec Dies" or "Regina Coeli" from time to time, since I loved to sing very much, there was no joy in my singing; at least not such a sense of jubilation as I had experienced when I lived alone with my mother. However, I offered it all to Jesus, hoping that better times would soon come.

> I was of a happy disposition, and I never liked crying of any kind.

Another reason for my sadness was the great worry that burdened our first spiritual director, Father Vincent. In February, soon after our foundation, many parishioners separated from St. Hedwig Parish, which he had organized, and formed an Independent Church. Because of these worries, Father Vincent became ill and was forced to leave Chicago for a short time. Since he was our confessor, he appointed his brother,[28] Reverend Joseph Barzynski, to substitute for him. Father Vincent returned at the beginning of April, a much weaker man. This proved to be a severe blow to us because he could not devote as much time and energy to us as our needs required.

> I offered it all to Jesus, hoping that better times would soon come.

---

28   St. Hedwig's Parish was founded in the year 1888. Its organizer was Reverend Vincent Barzynski, C.R. The first appointed pastor was Reverend Vincent's own brother, a diocesan priest, Reverend Joseph Barzynski. His assistant, Reverend Anthony Kozlowski, brought disunity to the parish by organizing an "independent" faction. Great dissension forced Father Barzynski, with the permission of Archbishop Feehan, to close the church. The remaining parishioners attended Mass at St. Stanislaus Kostka Parish.

The matter of the Polish National Church

Trouble was definitely in store for us. Sister Frances had a married sister, who joined the Independent Church. She begged to visit her frequently in order to bring her back to the Roman Catholic Church. After each visit she praised the fallen-away priest Kozlowski and his followers very much, and the other Sisters argued with her. I was forced to intervene and put a stop to the quarreling. Sister Frances was becoming more and more quarrelsome and disobedient. She even claimed that she was favored with visions and revelations. When she was asked to speak to Father Vincent about these apparitions, she balked at going to see him, saying that there was no necessity; that she knew all about him, etc. She strongly urged the other Sisters to leave the Community, and her purpose in doing so became quite apparent. In June she not only left the convent, but also joined the Independent Church and founded a community of Sisters there.[29]

Likewise, Sister Felixa's mother, who lived with us, showed marks of displeasure at the kind of life we were leading. She frequently reproached her daughter and coaxed her to look for a place of their own. The mother had been influenced to act this way by Sister Frances. Finally, she succeeded in winning her daughter over to her way of thinking, and they left at the beginning of June. It was a misfortune for Sister Felixa, for she never felt happy afterward. Following her mother's advice, she married; but later the mother was forced to leave the daughter's home. This marriage caused her more tears than smiles, and she often came to me in a very dejected mood to pour out her sorrows and to seek some consolation. She blamed her mother, whom she wanted to obey, for making her life so miserable.

"This Religious order will amount to nothing"

Before Sister Frances joined the Independent Church, she tried very hard to take the other Sisters along with her. She already influenced Sister Hyacinth; and they were planning to leave, stating that the Community would not prosper. They claimed that Father Vincent was very ill and would soon die, and nobody would then take care of the Sisters—and that

---

29 The group of alleged "independent" Sisters vanished rapidly enough since today not a trace of it is left.

would be the end of the foundation. Consequently, they did not see any purpose in working hard and giving their earnings to the Superior who, in their estimation, would later use that money for her own pleasure. Once, when Sister Frances received $40 in payment for the washing, both of them planned to keep the money and leave secretly. On second thought, however, they were ashamed to do it and handed the money over to me.

They disclosed what they had been planning to do to another Sister. I had not persuaded them to join, and I was not going to hold them back; they were free to do as they chose. I did notice, however, that our outlook on the Religious life differed greatly. They had another excuse for wanting to leave. Before we came to live together, Father Vincent had said that we were to be candidates on probation for six months, and after that time we would receive the habit of St. Francis. This stipulation had not yet been fulfilled, and our number of candidates was growing smaller. So when the Sisters would ask me if I knew when we would receive the habits, I would always say that we would get them when we really deserved them. These two were not satisfied with such an answer and left—Sister Hyacinth, to her mother; and Sister Frances, to Father Kozlowski, to whom she handed a check for $400, the original sum that she had deposited in the common fund at her entrance to our convent.

Whenever a Sister was ready to leave, I returned everything that she had brought in originally. According to the agreement which each of us made when we were organizing our little group, no one was to receive remuneration for the work that was performed. Money from this source was used for room and board and clothing.

"And I was left alone with Sister Angeline, Sister Josepha, and my mother ... we took a smaller apartment"

Only three of us remained from the original group: Sister Angelina, Sister Josepha, and I. My mother was the fourth person in the home. Since this building belonged to my sister at that time, she permitted us to take a smaller apartment on

> *We began again with renewed zeal and fervor. However, we needed more than that; we needed extra hands to help us... But God helped us here, too.*

the second floor. We began again with renewed zeal and fervor. However, we needed more than that; we needed extra hands to help us with all the wash that had to be done. But God helped us here, too.

Further difficulties

Our solicitous Father Vincent procured for us the use of the washing machines at the orphanage on Division Street. From the 5th of July we were allowed to do the washing there.[30] It was better, in a way, but it had its disadvantages, too. Since the orphanage had priority to the use of the machines in the earlier part of the week, we had no access to them until Thursday; we really had to hurry to complete our work in one day. Friday and Saturday were utilized for ironing, distribution of the clothes, and scrubbing the dining room at the rectory. Consequently, there was not enough time for the two of us to do all the work. So I hired a woman for the two days of the week, but even her help was insufficient.

All of a sudden, Sister Josepha began failing in health and I was obliged to send her to a doctor. This resulted in weekly visits and medication for her until October. I was the only one left who could stand the heaviest work because the lady whom I hired also complained that it was too hard for her to run the washing machines. Fearing that she, too, might become sick, I tried to relieve her as often as I could. And the Lord was helping me.

And the Lord was helping me.

Sister Josepha was hospitalized in the early part of October, leaving me with Sister Angelina who was engaged in sewing at home.[31] My mother did the cooking for us, and I hired one more woman to help me with the washing and ironing. Thus we continued working to attain the goal for which we had banded together.

We continued working to attain the goal for which we had banded together.

---

30   This pertains to an orphanage founded by Reverend Vincent Barzynski, that not long after was given to the community of Mother Theresa.
31   Sister Angelina was the only one to help, because Mother Anna still lived steadily with her family.

After three weeks of hospitalization, Sister Josepha returned home but she was unable to do any servile work. Within two weeks she was obliged to go back to the hospital to undergo surgery. The operation was successful, but she had to remain at the hospital for three additional weeks. When she returned, she was very weak and felt worse than ever before.

"I had no consolation whatsoever"

The most painful sorrow that I had to bear was Father Vincent's prolonged illness, which quite often compelled him to leave Chicago for the restoration of his health. His absence deprived me of all human consolation; even my closest companion was often depressed and gave vent to tears. In spite of everything, I did not lose my happy disposition and detected the Will of God in everything. I always kept in mind the predictions of Father Vincent; and since I had given my consent freely, my burdens became light and I never lost courage. I tried to continue working for this community most energetically.

> *In spite of everything, I did not lose my happy disposition and detected the Will of God in everything.*

> *Since I had given my consent freely, my burdens became light and I never lost courage. I tried to continue working for this community most energetically.*

Purchase of land in Avondale

And now I felt that the time had come for us to buy land for our future Home for the Aged and Crippled. After I had consulted with Sister Anna (Rose Wisinski) and Father Vincent, he suggested that we both go and look for a suitable site. After a long and fruitless search, we decided to ask a good friend of ours, Mr. Palubicki, for assistance. With his kind aid we finally found the lots on which our present buildings stand. We also asked him to advise us[32] on the type of building to construct for our intended

---

32 Here it concerns Avondale, at that time, a suburb of Chicago..

purpose. Mr. Palubicki, a professional bricklayer, willingly and kindly offered his assistance and found the architect with whom we later discussed the plans for the building.

We transacted the purchase of 12 lots for $5,000 on October 15, 1895. Having a saving of $100 at home, I gave it as a down payment. Then I had Mr. Kiolbassa[33] look over the papers of the agreement before we signed them. After the papers had been found in order, the land was recorded as sold to the two of us, namely, Rose Wisinski and me, on the 1st of November of that year. There was an initial payment of $1,000, leaving the remaining $4,000 as a debt to be remitted at the appointed time.

After the purchase transaction had been completed, we had something to look forward to; I redoubled my efforts in order to do as much as possible to save some money to meet the terms of the payment. The burden, however, rested mostly on me because Sister Anna had a bedridden mother who, for the past five years, was entirely helpless until she came to our new home. And Sister Anna, too, being of delicate health herself, could not help me as much as she desired. Therefore, she left it up to me to transact all business connected with that purchase and to settle everything as best as I could. She was trying strenuously, nevertheless, to help me financially in paying off the debt for the land.

Another difficulty beset me. I had some money invested in my brother's and sister's properties, and I expected that they would return it to me whenever we needed the money. To my disappointment, neither one was able to do so at the time of need. I asked Father Vincent to view the land that we had bought, but he refused to comply with our wishes due to his ill health. Shortly afterwards he left for Texas to regain some of his strength; again we were left as orphans without a Father. Luckily

> *We could only place our trust in God; to hope solely in Him was the safest course.*

---

33 Peter Kiolbasa held a high position in the administration of the city of Chicago.

enough, Father Simon, who was also good to us and well-disposed toward our cause, often consoled and encouraged me when the going was rugged. But he, too, became sick and had to spend several weeks in bed. Then I realized and saw that even in this instance we could only place our trust in God; to hope solely in Him was the safest course.

A dispute with a priest over payment

Soon I was to be confronted with another heart-breaking problem. Father Simon was the treasurer for the Resurrectionist Fathers at St. Stanislaus Kostka rectory, and during his illness he was substituted by another priest. On the day of payment he asked me how much we were receiving for washing clothes. When I told him that our salary was $40 a month, he thought that it was too much. He went to the other priests to verify the statement and to get an opinion whether the amount was too high. He finally decided that $25 was sufficient; I disagreed and tried to explain, as well as I possibly could, that it was absolutely impossible to do all that work for such a small payment. Dissatisfied with my insistence for proper remuneration, Father found some ladies in the parish who wanted work; he strongly urged them to take the job from us and do the washing for $25.

Painful experience

The women hesitated because they did not care to work for that amount; but finally three of them consented to accept the position. When I was notified that my services were no longer needed, I cried in secret, unnoticed by anyone except the Lord Jesus. I could not refrain from shedding tears, thinking that I took upon myself the responsibility of caring for the new Community and

> *When I was notified that my services were no longer needed, I cried in secret, unnoticed by anyone except the Lord Jesus.*

maintaining it by the labor of my own hands. And here, even the source of our income had been taken away. Even though Father knew the purpose of our organization and the cause for which we had been saving our earnings, that is, for a Home for the Aged and Crippled, he ignored us in permitting the other women to take the work from us. I considered his act unChristian and felt aggrieved toward him. Moreover, Sister Anna had been receiving $15 per month for mending clothes and this, too, was taken away from her. We were expected to wash and mend clothes for $30 a month.

Actually, Father had already told the women to come, but I informed him that I had been paid two months in advance by Father Simon since we needed money immediately for our payment of the land. But if he were willing to let me keep the $80 as a donation toward the new home, the ladies could start washing now; and we would forego working the two months for which we were paid. He quickly agreed to have us continue washing for the next two months, as long as were paid for it. In the meantime, Father Simon came back. He decided to keep us, but our salary was lowered to $35 per month.

Building committee and "welfare society"

However, life has a way of going on amidst the sorrows and joys that befall us. When Father Barzynski returned from Texas, he advised me to organize a committee to assist him in making plans for the new home. The first member to serve on that committee was Mr. Bielinski of 17th Street, the president of the Polish Roman Catholic Union. We owe him a debt of gratitude because he was the one who, next after Father Barzynski, did the most towards having our new home built. The second member was the Reverend John Radziejewski; the third, Mr. Polenz, also from St. Adalbert parish. They had even organized a society in that parish, under the patronage of St. Joseph, for the purpose of giving us financial aid. The following were the members of the committee from St. Stanislaus Kostka parish: The Reverend Vincent Barzynski, C.R., Mr. Gniot,[34] Mr. P. Kiolbassa, Mr. John Maca, and Mr. W. Jedrzejek.

---

34 John Gniot sought the hand of Josephine.

Foundress goes collecting

Prior to the first meeting of that committee, Father Vincent, promising to obtain for us the necessary permission, had advised us to take up a collection in the Polish parishes. It was the most difficult thing for me to tackle. I had never thought that it would ever be necessary for me to beg money for my own upkeep and also for the project to which I had dedicated my life.

> I had never thought that it would ever be necessary for me to beg money for my own upkeep and also for the project to which I had dedicated my life.

The collection for the new Home for the Aged and Crippled had been announced in St. Stanislaus Kostka parish toward the end of July, 1896. The crucial moment arrived, and I had to forget the resolutions that I had made in the past. Being naturally shy, I was formerly determined never to solicit the aid of others, even if I were dying from hunger. But this was not a problem for me to question; I was obliged to lead. Therefore, I began with Father Vincent, who offered me $15 from the Resurrectionist Fathers. After he gave me his blessing, he instructed me to accept all the money as a donation for the Home for the Aged and Invalids; and to accept all rudeness for myself. I was greatly inspired by these words.

> After he gave me his blessing, he instructed me to accept all the money as a donation for the Home for the Aged and Invalids; and to accept all rudeness for myself. I was greatly inspired by these words.

Another source of encouragement came to me from our own Community. A few months previously, Agnes D., a former nun, had joined us. While still in the convent, she had done some collecting before and somehow seemed to like the job. I needed all the encouragement that I could possibly get.

As yet, we had no religious garb; and many parishioners, who knew me through sixteen years of active participation in parish activities,[35] were inclined to think that I, not caring to work, was innovating new and mysterious projects as an excuse to beg for my own personal welfare. Many noble persons, however, were quite understanding and willingly gave their donations. That first collection in St. Stanislaus Kostka parish brought us $330. Adding to this sum, the money collected at two other parishes, St. John Cantius and St. Adalbert, totaled $450— a sum beyond my expectations. Father was also very pleased with the results. This money was entrusted to Mr. P. J. Gniot, the treasurer.

Father Vincent told Sister Anna and me to contact each gentleman personally, who had promised to be a member of the committee; and to invite him to attend a meeting that would be held at the rectory. It took a lot of courage on my part to do this since I was naturally shy, but, above all, since I had to go alone. I would have felt more at ease if Sister Anna were with me, but she was usually excused because of her sick mother. Attending the meeting, with all those gentlemen and priests present, frightened me quite a bit; I would have been happier if I were less timid. Father Vincent, however, knowing my nature, purposely placed all these obstacles in my way to overcome my pride.

The meeting took place in the latter part of September, and all the members of the committee

---

35 Josephine did personal volunteer work, decorating altars, taking care of church linens and ornaments, etc.

were present. Happily for me, Sister Anna was my companion at this special assembly.

The initial topic discussed and agreed upon at that meeting was my inquiry concerning the allocation of the money that we had collected. Sister Anna's sister Mathilda, wanting to loan us some money, withdrew $400 from the bank; and Mrs. Elizabeth Karnowski brought her savings of $150 for this same purpose. Our collection, plus the loan, totaled $1,000, which I wanted to use to pay off our debt on the lots. The committee gladly gave their approval for this proposition.

Matter of building home, financial problems

The next matter on the agenda was the consideration of a plan for the building. It was suggested at first to rent a larger apartment in order to accommodate more residents before the new building was to be constructed. At that time I had already accepted one aged lady and two cripples. This good lady, Frances Konkowski, was 100 years old when she was brought to our home on September 2, 1896, by Mr. Kielczynski of St. John Cantius parish. Reverend Piechowski and he joined the committee, but they never really became active members of the group.

On September 20 of the same year, I accepted a blind girl by the name of Josephine Gagala; and a little later, another girl, Theodosia T., who had a crippled hand and was unable to earn her own living. Having three people to support already, and with more destitute applying continually, there was nothing else left for us to do but to seek larger quarters.

Foundress' holy obstinacy to achieve her goal

When I reported this to the committee, they advised us to buy an old house and move it on the land that we had purchased. I objected on the grounds that it would cost too much to renovate such an old building and, furthermore, it would still be a temporary home. Sister Anna supported me in the matter. Father Vincent then spoke up. He asked, 'What do they want—a mansion or a palace?" He told us that we would do better to think about all the lowly tasks that must be performed around the sick and the aged, such as taking away bedpans, etc., and not thinking about a comfortable home. Hearing such remarks, we said no more; but the committee also abandoned its suggestion of buying an old house. Instead, they passed a resolution, authorizing us to rent a larger apartment and to accept more residents. They would wait and see how we would manage in our new quarters. On the following day, Sister Anna and I began our difficult search for a larger apartment. In accordance with Father's wishes, we had been very careful not to consider renting an apartment in a building of brick or stone construction. But, to our great disappointment, we could not find suitable quarters in a frame house. Mr. Lewandowski was putting up a new brick building on Ingraham Street; the apartments were just what we needed. Upon notifying Father that no other building was available, he consented to our renting the necessary quarters from Mr. Lewandowski. Although we had to wait till October for the completion of the building, we signed an agreement whereby we would take three apartments at $22.50 per month.

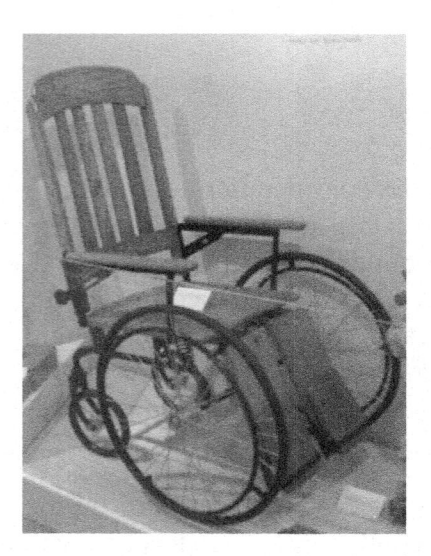

Second home near St. Stanislaus Kostka Church

We moved into our temporary quarters in the early days of November. I arranged sleeping accommodations for the residents, my mother, and myself on the main floor; another section of the same floor was to be our kitchen. The oratory, the Sisters' sleeping quarters, and workroom were on the second floor.

The observance of the daily program was the same as the former one. Spiritual reading, meditation, and prayers were said in common in the oratory in the morning, except on Thursdays, when we had to finish laundering the clothes. The residents said their prayers and rosary every evening on the first floor; and in the mornings they could attend Holy Mass in the nearby church. Also, the proximity of the parish buildings made it more convenient for us to do our work at the rectory. On Sundays we were privileged to be present at High Mass; a special pew was reserved for us in the lower church.[36] At 8:30 a.m. we read the Advanced Catechism in common, and in the afternoons we attended Vespers in church.

Year 1897

Flow of elderly ... Joey, legless orphan

After we moved in, I accepted a few more elderly women; no man had applied for admission thus far. A young boy[37] without legs was accepted in the early part of January. I taught him the catechism and prayers since he knew nothing of a religious nature. The first adult male, John Lewandowski, who was completely deaf, was accepted a year later.

---

36 Both churches, upper and lower, were overcrowded on Sunday.
37 Little is known about him, including his surname. He lived at Avondale for a few years and tradition tells us that he acquired a job as a switchman for a railway line.

> *Despite all the difficulties and troubles, I never felt completely exhausted. My greatest joy was when I knelt down to say the evening prayers and rosary with the residents and saw how fervently and willingly they participated in the religious exercises, although the situation was quite the reverse when they first came to us.*

Not just material aid, but especially spiritual aid

Despite all the difficulties and troubles, I never felt completely exhausted. My greatest joy was when I knelt down to say the evening prayers and rosary with the residents and saw how fervently and willingly they participated in the religious exercises, although the situation was quite the reverse when they first came to us. They resented going to church and, especially, to confession. Many had a deplorable habit of cursing, and I insisted strenuously that they get rid of that fault. When a few admonitions did not help, I threatened to expel anyone who did not cease cursing. This threat proved effective in each case. It seemed to me that God was pleased, even with the little good that I could do for His glory. Prior to the admission of these aged women, most of them had not attended church for many years.

> *It seemed to me that God was pleased, even with the little good that I could do for His glory.*

Indifference of committee

This had been a great encouragement to me to witness their improvement; but, on the other hand, I had to face complete indifference on the part of the members of the committee. They told us to get a larger apartment and to accept more residents;[38] they themselves sent in new charges, but none had ever bothered to ask if we had anything to eat. The money received from the collections had been turned over as a partial payment on the lots; but now we had to buy beds, bedding, furniture, and other indispensable necessities—not counting the rent, fuel, food, interest and tax.

"St. Joseph, our manager"—No money in the cashbox

With the exception of what we received every month from the relatives of the crippled boy, all the rest of the residents were charity cases. In spite of this, God was ever ready to help us. St. Joseph, too, who was chosen as the patron of our group and our project from its very inception, aided us in all our needs both temporal and spiritual. We never sought the help of God or St. Joseph in vain,[39] even though we did have to seek aid quite often.

> *God was ever ready to help us. St. Joseph, too, who was chosen as the patron of our group and our project from its very inception, aided us in all our needs both temporal and spiritual. We never sought the help of God or St. Joseph in vain, even though we did have to seek aid quite often.*

One day I had only one penny in the treasury when a Sister approached me and petitioned for a new dress. The one she presently wore was completely threadbare. The Sister was right, of course; undeniably, she needed a new dress. I explained the situation to her and promised to buy some material for dresses for all of us as soon as I would be able to do so. Not only was she dissatisfied with my explanation, but she was also annoyed by it to such an extent that she poured out all the grievances that she held against me in words full of anger. I was afraid that the good God might be offended by these words. When the Sister left me, tears welled into my eyes; and it seemed as though I could do nothing to hold them back. But I just had to do something for the poor Sister so that there would be peace again. Suddenly a thought came to me: "Doesn't St. Joseph care for us anymore?" I presented my problem to him and, with complete confidence in his assistance, I did not worry any more. Help

I firmly believe that St. Joseph would grant succor to anyone in need...

---

39   Mother M. Theresa fostered a special devotion to St. Joseph, as he is her baptismal patron saint.

actually came; I do not ascribe the result to my inadequate prayer, because I firmly believe that St. Joseph would grant succor to anyone in need—just as he did that day.

In the afternoon a lady came to see me. A few years ago, I sewed dresses for her daughters, as well as for others, before I had to take up washing. These women were disappointed that I would not personally sew for them, and they took their work elsewhere. I had some unhappy moments about this. In leaving me, this woman forgot to pay what she owed for the sewing. Now she not only paid the $6.40 that she owed, but added a fifty-cent donation since I had to wait so long for the payment. I was very grateful and sincerely thanked St. Joseph, to whom I attributed this unexpected help. I completely forgot that this money was still unreconciled until I actually saw the woman that day; but it all came back to me in due time.

And so the days were passing by, but sometimes it was very difficult. For example, when the number of the aged increased in the home, many a quarrel arose among them, as would happen with older people. News of such incidents even reached me at the orphanage[40] where I was busy with the washing. The Sister who was left in charge at home, instead of pacifying them, often drove them to louder bickering. Sometimes when I came home I could not even rest a bit after a day's hard work; I had to perform another job of bringing peace and quiet to the home again. At other times, the neighbors would also tell me about the noise emanating from our home. This hurt me deeply; but even in this instance it was necessary that I submit everything to the Will of God.

> *It was necessary that I submit everything to the Will of God.*

"I reminded Father Barzynski of the necessity to build."

In the spring I reminded Father Vincent about the plans[41] for the construction of the new building. He responded by telling me to invite the members of the committee for another meeting. Each gentleman promised

---

40 This is the already-mentioned orphanage on Division Street.
41 Spring of the year 1897.

to be present, except Father Piechowski,[42] who refused. No matter how I pleaded with him to come, it was all in vain. I knew how much Father Barzynski wanted him to be present, and I begged him for the favor with tears in my eyes; but I could not induce him to come. When I left the rectory with another Sister, I burst into tears and sadly told Father Barzynski that Father Piechowski could not come; but he wished us success in our venture. Father Barzynski, upon hearing about it, told me not to be disturbed; if Father Piechowski refused to come, the meeting would take place without him—and so it did. However, another problem troubled me. Sister Anna became ill, and I was compelled to appear at the meeting alone—among all those gentlemen and priests! This required much self-denial on my part; nevertheless, more embarrassment was in store for me at that meeting.

Matchmaking the foundress

After the preliminary points on the agenda were presented, Mr. Kiolbassa, looking at me, jestingly remarked: "Let's proceed differently in this matter. Our treasurer, Mr. Gniot, is a widower; it would be much easier to make wedding arrangements." All the men looked at me since I was the only woman there. I was terribly embarrassed and didn't dare raise my eyes. Father Barzynski, fully aware of my bashful nature and knowing my feelings on the matter, quickly came to my rescue. He remarked rather brusquely that such a conclusion did not require a meeting and discussion—there was a much more serious item on the agenda. No one dared to joke anymore, and all who were present concentrated on the subject under discussion. After many suggestions were proposed and evaluated, an architect was chosen with whom we were to consult and make plans for the building. These, in turn, were to be submitted to the committee for the final approval. We followed the instructions given, but the architect had to change his plans several times; Father Vincent felt that the building we wanted was too large for our purpose. Nevertheless, he eventually gave his approval to the final plans. These served as the basis for the construction of the present building of St. Joseph Home.

---

42 A Resurrection Father, John Piechowski, at first appointed as a lecturer of history and literature in Berlin, Canada (Kitschner,) in 1891 became rector of St. Stanislaus Kostka College. He was transferred to a newly organized parish of St. Hyacinth in Avondale; in 1895 he became pastor of St. Hedwig parish.

It wasn't, however, the last difficulty that we had to overcome. In the last six months Father Vincent had trouble with my sister, who was a prefect of the Rosary Sodality in our parish. She borrowed money from the parishioners to buy some property. Upon losing the ownership of two buildings, she was unable to repay the money. The same fate befell me since I also lent her money. A certain woman, who was the chief cause of the controversy, involved my name in the whole affair. She falsely stated that my sister[43] had given all that money to me; and that I, in turn, bought some lots on which a new house was to be built. News spread that in time my sister and her family would also move in and live in the new house.

Many people believed the false rumors. Among these was Mr. Jedrzejek, a member of the committee, to whom the woman told all these lies. As a result, he withdrew his membership from the committee. Then the storm, in all its fury, hit me. The persons, with whom I have lived in friendship for many years, turned against me. One day my closest and most sincere friend, Sister Anna, came to me and sorrowfully told me that she thought that nothing will come of the proposed building. Even Father Vincent was afraid to say anything.

"Everything conspired against me"

Considering her words, I just couldn't believe that what she said was true. I thought that as long as Father did not say anything about this to me personally, I won't believe that all our plans could have been dropped. I recalled his prediction made at the inception of our Community. He had foretold all this, although I never thought that it would ever reach such proportions. The facts spoke for themselves. Sometimes, however, I felt guilty that I caused the people to offend God by my actions. Father Vincent told me to put such thoughts completely out of my mind and encouraged me to continue working for the glory of God.

One day I had enough courage to ask Father Vincent directly what he thought about the plans for the new building. He received me very kindly and told me that he had difficulty in securing a loan. There was still a debt

---

43 This has reference to Mother's own sister, Rosalie. On June 15, 1873, she married Adam Frank. There were 13 children born of this marriage. In addition, Adam and Rosalie Frank adopted two orphan girls.

of $1,500 on the lots, and this debt had to be paid before a loan could be considered. Even in that event, none of the banks seemed interested in loaning us any money; but Father mentioned that he had a place where he probably might procure some help.

Josephine, superior of Rosary Confraternity, co-foundress of Arch-confraternity of the Immaculate Heart of Mary

I was so elated with the news that I did not know how I eventually got home. I resolved to do my utmost to pay off the debt on the lots as soon as possible. Without losing a moment, I called on Sister Anna to talk over the problem of finding the means to secure that much money.

"Nothing left for building"

We decided to approach the Women's Rosary Society and the Young Ladies Sodality and ask them for a donation since they had quite a bit of money in their treasury. We knew that Father Barzynski[44] would not object. The Rosary Society passed a resolution to donate a sum of $1,000, and the Young Ladies Sodality offered $500. This particular problem was settled, but we had nothing left for the building fund.

Shortly after, Father Vincent summoned Sister Anna and me to the rectory. When we arrived, he explained to us that in order to secure the necessary loan to start building, we must transfer the ownership of the lots to him. He already had a lawyer present, who would transact the business. He then would have to obtain the loan on his name because no one wanted to make the loan to us on our names. There was nothing else that we could do, except to agree to the proposed plan. This proposition would definitely benefit us greatly, and we had the lots transferred to Father Barzynski. He engaged Mr. Piotrowski, the attorney, to transact this business for us; and he did it immediately.

---

44   The archives of St. Stanislaus Kostka Parish, regarding the Arch-confraternity of Young Ladies, notes that the Superior of that division was Rose Wisinski. She performed that office until the year 1893. Prior to this time, Josephine Dudzik was chosen Superior of a second division, the present Mother M. Theresa.

Construction of St. Joseph Home begins

Work on the new building was to begin in the early part of September, 1897. According to the architect's plans, it was to be completed by Christmas; later developments proved that his deductions were incorrect. On the day of the groundbreaking, when Father asked us to pray fervently for the success of the venture, I trembled involuntarily with fear. I knew that it wouldn't be easy to learn how to be a good Religious. How could I impart such knowledge when I myself was ignorant and uneducated both in spiritual and secular matters? I considered myself a fool and recognized my need of education[45] in the proper techniques to guide others. Nevertheless, I only wished that God's Will be done; I placed all my trust in Him and would readily submit to His designs.

> *I only wished that God's Will be done; I placed all my trust in Him and would readily submit to His designs.*

On the other hand, it was a consolation to get away from the vicinity where we lived, and where many people misjudged and ridiculed us. How often I heard the remarks that nothing good will come out of our enterprise. More and more people doubted that this would actually happen. Now, however, they would find out that something was beginning to materialize after all—an institute for the aged and crippled would be built.

The digging and the laying of the foundation progressed very slowly, and it was not until the middle of October that the cornerstone was blessed. It was a private ceremony; only Father Barzynski, who performed the ceremony, and a few committee members were present. Actually, an ordinary weekday was chosen for the occasion. Neither Sister Anna nor I were present at the blessing of the cornerstone, but we saw the place sometime before that; and according to the size of the foundation, it seemed to us that the building would be much too small.

---

45 Mother completed few fundamental classes in a German school of her native town of Plocicz.

Foundress prays on rising of St. Joseph Home

At the beginning of November, I started out alone to see how far the work on the building had progressed. As soon as I was able to perceive the unroofed skeleton of the building, my heart was overwhelmed with that fear and joy which dissolved into gratitude toward God—the sentiments which He alone could understand. I then, ascended the ladder to the topmost section of this edifice in order to view the enterprise better and to pray. I was convinced that no one had seen me but God, to whom I felt so near. I was seized with a realization that this place, so distant from any church and people, was selected by Our Lord as the site of His dwelling; and that here, upon its altars, the Holy Sacrifice of the Mass would be celebrated. Steeped in these thoughts, I cried from joy.

Mother Anna, her parents, and sister live in Avondale

When Sister Anna and I had been making plans for moving into the new building, we were confronted with the problem of transferring her sick mother; she was bedridden, and the moving would have to take place in the winter season. Consequently, we resolved to rent an apartment near the location of the new building and move her mother before the cold days would set in. The moving into the new building could be taken care of more readily later. We rented a few rooms in a house on Ridgeway Avenue. This building now belongs to us. Sister Anna and her parents moved in on November 11, while her sister Mathilda stayed temporarily with her other sister[46] in Chicago. The dwelling, however, proved to be uncomfortable, especially for the aged couple. Their neighbors, who were Swedes, seemed to dislike the Poles and did nothing to stop the damage done to their property by the children. We decided that it would be best if Sister Anna's parents left this place. They moved into one of our buildings, which had been completed as a stable for the horse and cows. However, in one section which was utilized

---

46 Mathilda remained in care of Mother Anna.

as a storage room, the walls were plastered and a chimney was attached to it so that a stove could be conveniently installed. They moved into this room with all their belongings. Sister Anna also brought her chickens from Chicago. She and her parents not only bore all unimaginable inconveniences, but at times even the necessities of life were lacking.

There was no grocery store in the neighborhood, and the closest one was on Milwaukee Avenue. But with no transportation available, this was no help. Even when Sister Anna and her parents were snowbound, it was necessary to walk that distance in order to reach the store; they had no one to bring them food. All three of them were in poor health; and instead of living there a month, as had been expected, they actually stayed in that stable for four months. Life here was quite similar to the one led by the Holy Family in the cave in Bethlehem. And the rest of us, who were supposed to move into our new quarters before Christmas, were unable to do so until March 23. As soon as winter began, the workers lingered at their work and were not mindful of the time for its completion. Father Vincent lived a distance away and was too weak to oversee them; as a result, they would not obey others.

> Life here was quite similar to the one led by the Holy Family in the cave in Bethlehem.

Year 1898

I am reverting again to our Community, which increased in number as soon as the news spread about the construction of the home. The girl with the crippled hand, whom I accepted as a resident a year before, went in January of that year to the hospital to undergo surgery on that hand. The operation proved successful, and when she returned to us she was able to perform all the necessary work with that hand. She pleaded to be accepted to the Community, and her petition was granted; she entered on November 21. Also one of the young ladies of the Rosary Sodality applied for admission as a convalescent, although her desires, as she later revealed, were to join the Community. She wanted to see for herself what kind of life the Sisters had been leading. She felt entirely at home with us.

New vocations - Sisters Clara and Elizabeth

There were two new candidates since the feast of the Presentation—Theodosia T. and Maryann Ogurek.[47] The third one, Caroline Baut,[48] who entered on December 7, was a member of the Third Order of St. Francis. Consequently, there was already now a bigger group which consisted of seven members, and Sister Anna was the eighth. Three years ago, on the feast of the Immaculate Conception, the number was the same. Later, some left; and again the number remained the same as had been at the time of moving into the new home. It always happens that God sends sorrow, but He also sends consolation.

> *It always happens that God sends sorrow, but He also sends consolation.*

The number of the aged and crippled also increased, and by January, 1898, there were fifteen—twelve women and three men. But two of the women did not want to leave Chicago, and they preferred to stay with their relatives rather than come with us. Slowly, the time drew near when it was necessary to bid farewell to Chicago, such a pleasant place, and especially to the church of St. Stanislaus Kostka in which the Lord Jesus bestowed so many great graces upon me. Nevertheless, I didn't feel too bad, knowing that such is the Will of God; and that He would continue to enrich me with His graces if I only would continue to co-operate with Him and benefit spiritually from His goodness.

> *Nevertheless, I didn't feel too bad, knowing that such is the Will of God; and that He would continue to enrich me with His graces if I only would continue to co-operate with Him and benefit spiritually from His goodness.*

---

47   Maryann Ogurek, Sister M. Clara, was born in Makovrarsk on May 6, 1875. She entered the Community on November 21, 1897 and died on December 8, 1909.
48   Caroline Baut, Sister M. Elizabeth, entered on December 7, 1897 and died on June 18, 1960.

Farewell to St. Stanislaus Kostka, move to Avondale

On the vigil of St. Joseph, the patron and master of our home, I tried to get all the aged and Sisters to go to confession, with the exception of one cripple, who did not receive his First Holy Communion. On the feast of St. Joseph, all received Holy Communion with the intention of obtaining blessings on this new household which we were to occupy on March 23. On that day I went to buy a cooking stove and all the essential items for the kitchen with Mr. Gniot, the treasurer of the Committee of Financial Aid to us. I also purchased food from his store, where he had been a clerk at that time. He promised to haul some of the furniture from the old quarters to the new home, and he really kept his promise.

Difficulties in supporting the elderly and crippled

What great difficulties I was exposed to during this moving! Father Vincent suggested that I should rent a big wagon in which all things could be moved at once. No one, however, wanted to serve us because there was excessive mud in the vicinity due to lack of streets. Except for the stretch on Milwaukee Avenue, the other areas were hazardous. I asked a few of the businessmen, Mr. John Thiel and Mr. Gniot, for assistance. The former offered his services and his horse and wagon, and moved our things during the entire day. Even though his horse was very tired, he paid no attention and kept on using him as long as possible. He saw the necessity of our being moved in one day. Mr. Gniot also permitted his horse and wagon to be used; the third wagon and horse belonged to us. They were in our possession for some time already, and my brother Joseph was the chief driver.

And so the Lord helped us to move successfully, but again we were faced with a new tribulation. It was the shortage of bread and other foods

> *And so the Lord helped us to move successfully...*

which could not be obtained in larger quantities, to meet the needs of our aged and Sisters. The bakers did not deliver bakery goods to the homes, and the only grocery store in our neighborhood was unprepared to supply our needs. The source of worry for me during the first week was to procure enough food for everybody. Sister Anna joined us also at this time with her parents. There were, therefore, eight Sisters and fifteen aged cripples. Another worry was that we could not get coal here, and no one wanted to deliver it from the city on account of the bad roads. It was quite cold, and it continued to be so for over a month. Again my brother Joseph helped us by delivering the coal from time to time, disregarding all the inconveniences in performing this job. He almost killed the horse with this strenuous work; after that the animal was no longer fit for the work.

The third trouble which weighed heavily on my mind was the lack of means of earning a living. When we left Chicago, we also abandoned our services in doing the laundry for the people; it was our chief source of income. Here we had no appropriate place for the laundry, or a way to make deliveries. We had some sewing to finish on orders which we took while we still lived in the city. It was our desire to continue this type of work in the future, but our new place was situated too far from the people for the purpose of giving us new orders. Our present neighborhood consisted of a few persons who had been giving us orders for some work, but it was not enough to support twenty-three persons. Again, God had not forsaken us in these tribulations.

Except for the neighborhood grocery store, there were no other stores around, and one had to drive to town to purchase a supply of home necessities. I was forced to go shopping quite often for my big family with Sister Josepha. Since there was no transportation available, except by horse and wagon, I had to buy the wagon, and the horse was donated to us by St. Stanislaus Kostka rectory. We had, however, no coachman. Our residents, three aged men, could not help us. Two were too weak to drive, the third one did not know how.

Foundress in the role of carpenter

The only alternative, therefore, was to take over the driving by my steady companion or me. Although Sister Josepha was physically weak, she was bold enough to drive when it became a necessity. I accompanied her whenever she drove, regardless of the difficulty which I encountered because of the tremendous amount of work that I had to do at home. In general, I had to undertake everything that needed to be done on our property; but I tried to do the best I could. Being insufficiently skilled in carpentry work, I bruised my hands many times while doing the work that had to be finished here and there.

Dedication of St. Joseph Home

The arrangements for the blessing of our home were made for the 1st of May. It was Father Vincent's suggestion to have it on the feast of the Solemnity of St. Joseph. He was under the impression that it would fall, as usual, on the third Sunday after Easter. The feast of the apostles, Sts. Philip and James, fell on May 1, and it could not be transferred. Consequently, the feast of the Solemnity of St. Joseph was postponed to the following Wednesday.

First Mass in the first home owned by the Community

The blessing of our home,[49] nevertheless, took place on May 1 since everything had been arranged. The Holy Sacrifice of the Mass had been celebrated in our little chapel for the first time on that day, although we had no Blessed Sacrament reserved until a year later. In the afternoon Father Barzynski performed the ceremony of the blessing of our Home; he was assisted by Father Sedlaczek, who was pastor of St. Hyacinth Church and also our temporary confessor. Father Barzynski delivered a very inspiring sermon to the guests[50] who assembled for the dedication. The ceremony had

---

49 The original name given to this residence was "Home of St. Joseph's Asylum."
50 The first chapel in St. Joseph Home was so small that barely 20 persons could fit in it.

to be held outdoors because of the large number of people whom we were unable to accommodate in our small building. The collection, which was taken during the service, amounted to $60. In the presence of Father Vincent, I submitted the money to Mr. Gniot, the treasurer of the Committee.

Management problems — "How to feed this crowd?"

I intended to use the money collected to pay for the cow, which I bought shortly before the dedication for $31. I wanted to treat the guests with fresh milk and also to defray the expense for food. I was perplexed, however, when Father Vincent told me to entrust the money to Mr. Gniot. I told Father that, for the first time, I am in need of money. He advised me to go to the rectory to his assistant, Father Andrew Spetz, and ask him for some money. He gave me only $40, and I would have needed at least $100. Nevertheless, how could one take more if more were not given? I would have to manage with the amount I received.

Sister Anna and I decided that it was necessary to buy another cow since we noticed that there was a shortage of milk. It would be quite economical to have more cows because the cost of fodder in our locality was very low during the summer. Fortunately, someone returned a debt of $50 to Sister Mary Anna, and she loaned the money to me. One day Sister Anna and I went to the Chicago stockyards and bought a cow and two small pigs for that amount. Then, too, we had some chickens which Sister Anna brought with herself from Chicago; we had enough food provisions for the present.

On May 19, the Notre Dame Sisters from the orphanage[51] brought Angela Osinski, a crippled girl, to us. At the beginning of June we got another aged woman from Avondale, thus increasing the number of people

---

51   This is the same orphanage near Division Street.

to feed and clothe; and there was almost no source of income from anywhere; it was undeniable, however, that St Joseph remembered us in so many instances. In some way we made a living during the coming months, even though the hardships seemed to increase from day to day. The problem was quite evident that I would, seemingly so, never be relieved of the constant worry about the manner and means of sustaining ourselves here. The first candidate who applied for admission at the new place was Antoinette G. I did not have the desire to accept her since I considered her unsuitable to the Religious life. Fearing the problem of feeding an additional person, I was reluctant to admit her. But on the recommendation of Father Vincent I received her; however, she remained with us only a short time.

> St. Joseph remembered us in so many instances.

After serious deliberation on how to sustain and feed my charges, I thought of dressing some of the Sisters as postulants and sending them to solicit alms. Up to this time we still wore secular clothes. Father Barzynski accepted the idea; but, unfortunately, we had no driver to take the Sisters to the various market places. Suddenly I recalled that I had a relative in Milwaukee, WI, who spent some time in a mental institution, but presently was well enough to be released. Father Vincent consented to his coming, but Father Sedlaczek had some doubts about him. Acting upon the approval of Father Vincent, Sister Anna and I went to Milwaukee and brought him to our home on August 2. Now he was our driver, carpenter, and engineer; that made matters much easier for us.

When the candidates went on their first soliciting venture on August 6, they returned with $16 and plenty of food supplies. My troubles ceased; I had no more doubts or worries about how or where to obtain the quantity of food needed for the large family which had been constantly increasing. On July 30 we accepted an aged woman, Mrs. Lagodzinska, who brought $250 and deposited it with Father Vincent.

In our garden we planted a great variety of vegetables which yielded an abundant harvest. We also had plenty of milk from our two cows; sometimes, even too much.

Catherine G., (Sister Josepha) who helped me very much with my work, left the Community on September 14 since she did not possess the qualifications required of a nun. Antoinette G., who entered in June, also returned to the world and later married. As if to replace her, Anna Welter,[52] the present Sister Mary, entered the Community on the following day, August 15.

Dismissal of Foundress from office - Oct. 4, 1898

A change of the Superior took place in our Community on October 4, 1898. In the morning of the feast of St. Francis, Father O. Rapacz celebrated Holy Mass. In the afternoon Father Vincent asked us to assemble in the chapel, and there he appointed Sister Mary Anna as Superior; he received Mary Ogurek and Anna Welter to the Third Order of St. Francis. Mary received the name of Sister Mary Clara; and Anna, the name of Sister Mary. They retained these names in religion.

> *I still felt like a fish removed from water without the presence of the Blessed Sacrament.*

Now that the burden was taken away from me, it suddenly seemed as though a heavy stone fell from my head; and very often I perceived unusual happiness. On the other hand, however, I still felt like a fish removed from water without the presence of the Blessed Sacrament. The nearest church was on Milwaukee Avenue, and that was quite a distance from us. During the summer we attended Holy Mass whenever we were able, although all of us could not attend it daily. The situation became more intense during the winter months when the roads were practically impassable. At times I felt such a great yearning for Jesus

---

52 Anna Welter, later Sister Mary, died in the Community on October 17, 1955.

> *At times I felt such a great yearning for Jesus in the Blessed Sacrament that I was ready to run to church, even late in the evening.*

in the Blessed Sacrament that I was ready to run to church, even late in the evening. I believe this yearning was just a temptation. Father Vincent suggested that I should think about my residents and not dream. As much as I tried to follow his advice, the longing for Jesus would persist and return often.

> *The longing for Jesus would persist and return often.*

Reverend Andrew Spetz steps into life of new Community

In the same month I submitted a financial account of all the years when I was in charge. Now I was free from the entire burden. In reference to our life in common, we did not as yet have any Rule to follow in the Religious life. But Father Andrew,[53] being solicitous about our Community, noticed this need. He drew up the Constitution with the assistance of Father Vincent, who was still ailing and could not take care of us as he so desired. Father Andrew brought a copy and told us to regulate the manner of our life accordingly. It became evident that many points had not been stated clearly, and some were impractical. After the Constitution had been revised several times in accordance with the latest rules of the Church, each Sister received a copy so that she would adapt and conform herself to the observance of the principles. That was in 1909.

"It was my favorite holyday."

I am returning again to where I had left off previously. The feast of the Immaculate Conception of the Blessed Virgin was approaching. It was the anniversary of the founding of our Community, and at an opportune time I reminded Father Vincent that we will be celebrating this feast in our home for the first time. I questioned him in regard to the manner of how we

---

53 Father Andrew Spetz took over the spiritual direction of the Community upon the death of Reverend Barzynski.

should observe it. He answered that we should make a novena, as we had done formerly, and observe a week of retreat. He also mentioned that the postulancy would begin from this feast. Father Vincent promised to give us a few conferences and asked us to remain recollected during this time.

First Postulancy in the new Community

Since this was our first retreat, we had no conception of what would be expected of us besides complying to the rule of silence and attending Father Barzynski's conferences. Truthfully, we were delighted at the thought of beginning our postulancy; and I was so overwhelmed by it that I wished to honor my favorite feast of the Mother of God more solemnly. I began to plan for the celebrations of this feast and also for the approaching Christmas festivities.

> *Truthfully, we were delighted at the thought of beginning our postulancy; and I was so overwhelmed by it that I wished to honor my favorite feast of the Mother of God more solemnly.*

First Christmas in new home ... no organ

After the retreat and novena had begun, a few members of the St. Stanislaus Kostka Church Rosary Sodality visited us on Sunday. Prior to their coming, a thought came to my mind during the retreat meditations, and I considered it very beneficial. It was about obtaining an organ so that we could, here in this deserted place and in our home, play and sing together at Midnight Mass in honor of the Child Jesus so that we could thank Him for all the graces, but especially because He led us to this peaceful environment, as if it were a desert retreat, from the Babylon of Chicago[54]. I made my meditation known to Sister Superior so that these members would be asked to purchase an organ. I even envisioned Sister Clara's going to Brother Adalbert[55] for instructions in order to be able to play by Christmas. What a

---

54 She is referring to downtown Chicago.
55 Brother Adalbert Goralski was a Resurrectionist.

concept I then had about music! I was certain that she would learn to play by that time.

> *It (my thought) was about obtaining an organ so that we could, here in this deserted place and in our home, play and sing together at Midnight Mass in honor of the Child Jesus; so that we could thank Him for all the graces…*

Sister Superior gladly confirmed my petition and mutually shared my opinion. As soon as I asked the ladies for the organ, they immediately consented and agreed wholeheartedly. They said, however, that they must first go and ask Father Vincent for his sanction and permission. I was most confident that he would agree, and I even imagined that the organ was already ours. Just as soon as the ladies mentioned the petition to Father, he laughed and said: "I will give them an organ! They are to make a retreat, and here they are longing for music, and yet a Religious Brother should teach them music!" And he made known to them that on the following day he would come to us for a conference.

Nevertheless, I found out the results concerning the organ before Father Vincent came for the conference; the ladies informed us about what he had to say concerning the matter. I was, therefore, already prepared, but not the least sorry for my action. As soon as Father came for the conference and began to talk, but not as sternly as he threatened, he expressed himself jokingly. He mentioned that he understood well that we were yet like children in the Religious life, and, as a result, did not take it as a great transgression. I went to him after the conference and apologized; he was very considerate and gave me some instructions, which later became useful. He also told me that he would see to it that Sister Clara would be able to learn music if she would have the desire for it, but not from the Brother. So he recommended Mr. Wiedemann, then Mr. Kwasigroch, and lastly, Mr. Kwasigroch's daughter. But here it ended, and my first choice was fulfilled; almost a year later Brother Adalbert taught music to our Sisters. He was their main instructor and continued to be so whenever it was necessary.

But as for Christmas, we remained without an organ! The thing that saddened us still more was that on the vigil of Christmas, Father Andrew came to hear our confessions instead of Father Vincent. How startled we were because he had never administered the sacrament of confession to us before—only Father Sedlaczek or Father Vincent. Furthermore, we thought that he already turned us over to Father Andrew but it was not so. On Christmas Day he came and celebrated a Low Mass, and we were again very consoled that he did not forsake us completely.

But I am returning to our retreat, which ended with a general confession. I remember that I was very moved and, as much as I noticed, the other Sisters were also.

Conflicts that led to the dismissal of Foundress

On the feast of the Immaculate Conception, Father Vincent celebrated Holy Mass; we received Holy Communion and were very happy. After a short sermon, he told us that with this day we were starting our postulancy; however, it was very hard. It was difficult primarily because we were to train ourselves to live according to the Rule[56] but, at the same time, we were so distracted in criticizing one another, gossiping, suspecting, and misjudging, and the like. The shortcomings in our conduct became more evident when we moved to our new home.

Father Vincent told me that I should give these Sisters some time to rejoice and not to worry so much about silence. Even though the order of the day was somewhat modified, I endeavored to observe it because I considered that advancement in the spiritual life would result from adhering to this practice. It wasn't too difficult since there had been such a small number of us at that time, and whoever entered tried to conduct herself according to the Rule. But as soon as the Rule was observed less rigidly, it was then difficult to lead back to that original order. Consequently, it was always worse for me because I remembered the promises which I had made. I was not able to look peacefully on such a life and, for my part, tried to encourage the observance of the Rule in keeping silence as before. Because of this good example, I brought upon myself great displeasure from almost every Sister—that I am not a Superior and try to rule; that I have nothing to say about this.

---

56 This text unintentionally becomes enlightenment to the conflict, which resulted in the removal of Mother from the position of Superior.

I tried to bear these jeers patiently at home, although at times misunderstandings and quarrels were the consequence. However, when the Sisters went for collection, they spread rumors and began to talk among the people about my conduct. As soon as I found out about this, I decided that I cannot have this person, who does such things, as my Sister. Truthfully, and according to my sister, the soliciting Sisters had to bear derisive remarks from the people frequently.

> I tried to bear these jeers patiently at home, although at times misunderstandings and quarrels were the consequence.

Accusation before Father Barzynski

And so these remarks, although enunciated in an entirely different meaning, were carried to Father Vincent. He called me to himself in the presence of Sister Superior and another Sister. The one, however, who spread false rumors, left the Community. I was then the only one who was scolded and admonished. I thought and resolved that I would never again make any reprimands, and that I would let them do whatever they wished. Instead of it being better because we had the Rule, it had been getting steadily worse. I had been looking at this laxity with astonishment and wondered whether it is possible for life to be like this in a convent.

Finally a violent temptation came upon me, and I was bothered with these thoughts: "How foolish you are! Couldn't you have remained quietly with your mother and served God better and accomplished more good than now? In this way of life you might condemn yourself because you can't live here as the Rule prescribes, nor can you observe the Commandments of God. Here you will condemn yourself...." These thoughts spun through my mind, and it seemed to me that everything would dissolve into pieces. Already it appeared as if all were going away. "When this would actually materialize," I thought, "I'll be able to manage anywhere."

Beginning of the Night of the Soul for Foundress

Although I had submitted my money toward the payment of the lots, I came to the conclusion that I would not take anything from here. I would earn as much anywhere for my mother and my own meager support; I never liked to dream about conveniences. And I would reassure myself, as much as I was able, thinking that whatever I did I wanted to do it for the greater glory of God. And if God did not demand further work from me, I would agree to His wishes.

This blissful peace, however, did not last for long. The promises, which were made to Father Vincent and to God in the early stages of the enterprise, resounded in my heart. I recalled when Father said that perhaps I would be solicitous about this Community as long as everything would go well—maybe one year, and maybe two, and maybe even ten. But as soon as obstacles would arise, then I would become discouraged and forsake everything. Father remarked that in this way I would bring him and myself to scorn, and also the Church which permits such trials. Most of all, I would deceive those persons whom I would accept. But I promised God and him, after some deliberation, so long as I would live I would try, as much as my strength would endure, not to give such scandal.

And here, again, a new struggle ensued as soon as I considered the promises. How would I be able to manage this? We did not have a steady confessor to whom I would be able to present my troubles. The only thing that I could do, I thought to myself, was to pray that God would change all of this. Therefore, I began to present our difficulties to Jesus more often in order to expect help from Him only.

Year 1899

Father Barzynski visits the Sisters for the last time

We could no longer expect great help from Father Vincent. We were almost forsaken. On January 23, namely on the day of the espousal of the Blessed Virgin Mary, he came and celebrated Holy Mass and heard our confessions. After Holy Communion, these various temptations departed somewhat from me. On this particular day Father was unusually happy. He brought the chalice, enclosed in a case, to us, in the celebration of the Holy Sacrifice of the Mass. He joked with us, consoled us, and departed. Who would expect that this was the last Mass which he would celebrate for us! And it was actually so. Upon his return from our home he almost met with a tragic accident as he alighted from the streetcar on Division Street. It was a hair-breadth miracle that he was not run over by another streetcar approaching from the opposite direction. When he regained consciousness, he became so very ill that almost everyone said that he would not live long. Nevertheless, I could not even think of his leaving us already—we still needed him very much. It was a painful blow to us. The people, on the other hand, also blamed us since he got sick while returning home from our residence, that we brought him grief, and they continued with other similar talk. We were, however, peaceful about all these accusations; we did not feel guilty.

And the Lord helped Father Vincent to regain his consciousness. He was recovering his health, although not completely, because he was very weak. Soon the Lord had so ordained that he permitted him to visit us once more on St. Joseph Day. Father Andrew, considering that he is at least quite strong, gave him a surprise. He hired a wagon and told him to get ready because they would go for a ride. Both of them came to us, a visit from which he gained great delight. We, too, could not contain ourselves from joy, but that joy was to be only a brief one. After Father Vincent gave us a short conference, I humbly begged him for admission to the Novitiate. He answered that it might be sooner than I expected. I was overwhelmed with the news, and I later conveyed it to the other Sisters. The joyous announcement made them all happy. This was to be Father's last visit before his death. God did not forsake or forget us because He sent the Reverend Father Andrew, a good, solicitous and mindful Father for the good of our Community. He saw the failing health and incapability of Father Vincent and became more interested in the welfare of our Community.

> God did not forsake or forget us...

Through Father Vincent's efforts, the establishment of a Novitiate was made possible; and with its beginning we were to have the Blessed Sacrament in our chapel. That was a privilege for which we were very delighted. As I had already mentioned previously, the distance to church was great; during the severe winter I was not able to be in church for two weeks. Consequently, it was lonely for us, but we understood that the Lord sent this inconvenience upon us.

> We were to have the Blessed Sacrament in our chapel. That was a privilege for which we were very delighted.

Father Barzynski is hospitalized

Two weeks after Father Barzynski visited us, he became worse. He was taken to the Alexian Brothers Hospital, from whence he never returned. On his feast day, that is April 15, Sister Anna and I received permission from Father Andrew to visit him. Neither of us would have thought that this would be our last meeting. We were going to have reception to the Novitiate on the feast of the Solemnity of St. Joseph; but Sister Anna, the Superior, postponed the date to the Feast of the Ascension because she feared that Father Vincent was too weak. She expected him to be much stronger by then, but he died before that feast. Unfortunately, he could not have the pleasure of investing us in the religious garb as he had hoped. Had it not been for the postponement, he would have made it on the day set originally, because he had been feeling exceptionally well that morning. He even arose, dressed himself, and awaited the arrival of the carriage, but he was soon notified about the change in dates.

Death of spiritual director

On the morning of May 2, we received the news about our beloved Father, which told us there was no hope for his recovery. On the previous day, one of his parishioners, Mr. Stanislawowski, a prominent citizen, took him for a ride in the park. He caught a cold, contracted pneumonia and, because of his already weak condition, there was no possible help for him. We all became alarmed at the news. It seemed to me as if someone shot an arrow through my heart. I lost all hope of my seeing him at least once more. During the day we anxiously had been looking forward to hearing something about his condition, but no news reached us until the following morning. While reciting our morning prayers, we heard the church bells tolling for a deceased person. I knew, as if someone were telling me, that it was for our dear spiritual Father. The other Sisters felt likewise, and nobody could convince us that we might have been mistaken.

"The greatest grief experienced in my life"

On the way to church for Mass we were told that Father Vincent died.[57] I cannot express our sorrow. We all began crying almost aloud and when we reached the church our weeping redoubled. To me this was the greatest sorrow I had experienced in my life. My present grief was greater than when my parents died, whom I had loved dearly. We needed Father Vincent all the more now since we still did not have the religious garb. We were busily preparing it and also hoping to have received it from his hands. Besides, there were many other reasons for our feeling of abandonment.

---

57   Father Vincent died May 2, 1899.

"My confessor guided me"

I felt the loss of a good spiritual Father who, for almost sixteen years, was my confessor. After God and the Mother of God, I owed the greatest gratitude to him. My success, while still in the world, was due to his directing me on the road of self-denial. His exemplary life of mortification, the great love of neighbor, and also the other virtues which shone during his life, and which I observed for so many years, now disappeared with him forever.

Heroic submission to Divine Providence

But this is my only consolation in knowing that I did not place my hope in him, as almost everyone suspected. I tried to conform to his advice not to place any confidence in him but in God. If it were to the contrary, then it would have also been the end of our Community—as so many people thought. However, we did not waver but had hope in God; since God began this work through this priest, He would continue it for His glory.

> We did not waver but had hope in God...

Funeral of Father Barzynski—"What will these old maidens do now?"

The funeral took place on May 5, 1899, and almost all of us attended. We entrusted our home and the aged to the care of Our Lord, and we traveled to church by streetcar. On the previous day some of us had been present at the exportation of the body from the rectory to the church. It was still a consolation to us that we were admitted, in spite of the huge crowd which was unable to get inside. The priests, Sisters in religion, and guests occupied the center aisles, and we were fortunate to be seated with them. Through the kindness of the church committee who knew us, we were the recipients of that much-appreciated privilege. There we could pray and weep.

After the remains were carried out from the church, we walked slowly on the sidewalk alongside the body. On passing the orphanage, almost every orphan was outdoors bidding farewell with tears in his eyes for his Father and guardian. Again new sadness embraced us at the thought of what would happen with these orphans. We knew with what difficulties this orphanage was founded and how much Father suffered on this account. And so we walked up to Milwaukee Avenue and then took the streetcar to Jefferson Park; from there we walked to the cemetery. We had to walk at a fast pace in order to arrive before the funeral cortege. When we came to the designated place, we stood at a short distance from the grave. We were not able to get closer to see the coffin once more since there were many priests, Sisters, and prominent people. After the eulogy, the prescribed prayers and singing, the coffin was lowered and covered with earth—just as every poor mortal is buried. During these ceremonies many eyes were turned in our direction, and many people pointed us out to their friends. Some pitied us and wondered what would happen now. Others again smiled at us saying, "What will become of these old maidens now?" etc. However, after everyone departed, we approached his grave, and with tears we bid him farewell and left the cemetery. And although we all felt very tired, we headed toward home on foot and offered this mortification for his soul.

A short distance from our home we were met by one of our residents, who was waiting for us to give us an account of things during our absence. The cows had run away, but were found again; and Mrs. Lagodzinska, a resident, also left and did not return. The thought that brought about the greatest fear to the old folks was that as soon as we would return from the funeral, we would ask them to leave. They were almost positive about that, but such a thought had never occurred to us. It was necessary to forget the sorrow and to occupy ourselves with a greater energy with our husbandry and charges.

> *It was necessary to forget the sorrow and to occupy ourselves with a greater energy with our husbandry and charges.*

"Providence sent us another Father"

After the loss of Father Vincent, the Providence of God, as I mentioned previously, had sent us another Father in the person of the Reverend

Andrew Spetz. He alone, perhaps, was able to understand this untold sorrow which burdened our hearts.

Confirmation of Community, Constitution, and opening Novitiate

Father Spetz tried earnestly to vest us in our religious garb. He wrote our Constitution while Father Vincent was still alive, and obtained its approval. He was also instrumental in having the Ordinary, the Most Reverend Archbishop Patrick Feehan, approve our Community and grant us permission to begin our Novitiate.

After some deliberation with Father Andrew, the formerly designated day on which we were to begin our Novitiate was transferred to May 21, the forthcoming celebration of the Descent of the Holy Spirit. We tried to prepare for this day as best as we knew and understood. We made a four-day retreat under the guidance of the Reverend Florian Matuszewski. Through his conferences we obtained a greater knowledge of convent life, and thus we were prepared for our Novitiate much better than for the postulancy. Although we had no substitutes to take over our daily duties, we tried our very best to devote more time to spiritual exercises and to prepare for this moment so desired by us. I couldn't contain my joy at the thought that from this day we would have the Blessed Sacrament in our small chapel.

> *I couldn't contain my joy at the thought that from this day we would have the Blessed Sacrament in our small chapel.*

Blessed Sacrament in tabernacle — first time

On the eve of Pentecost, our good Father brought the ciborium for the Blessed Sacrament. When we saw that, we somewhat forgot about our grief which momentarily withdrew but returned anew. We knew that now we would be able to associate more

> *Now we would be able to associate more frequently with the Lord Jesus, so close in our midst, and present our various anxieties to Him.*

frequently with the Lord Jesus, so close in our midst, and present our various anxieties to Him.

Our Lady of Victory Statue

We had our chapel quite well furnished. When we moved about a year ago, we received a statue of Our Lady of Victory,[58] donated by the Young Ladies of the Immaculate Heart of Mary Sodality from St. Stanislaus Kostka Church. There was also a statue of St. Joseph from Mr. Breszman; a statue of St. Francis from Mr. Kaczmarek; and two large framed pictures which I received from the Young Ladies Rosary Sodality on my feast day. The pews were donated by the Women's Rosary Sodality from St. Stanislaus Kostka Church on the occasion of the Golden Wedding Jubilee of Sister Anna's parents. The altar came as a gift from the Sodality Chapel of St. Stanislaus Kostka Church. We already had the most necessary equipment in the chapel, but the most important gift was received on the day of our Novitiate—the Blessed Sacrament.

Foundress begins Novitiate

As I already mentioned, we received the religious habit from the hands of Reverend Andrew Spetz on Pentecost Day at 7:30 a.m. The ceremony of our investiture was celebrated in the following manner: we walked into the chapel, and each one had the folded garb before her in the first pew. Father intoned the Veni Creator, and we sang it together with him. He then blessed our garb, spoke to us in appropriate words for this occasion, placed the religious garb in our hands, and then we departed to an adjoining room to dress. Sister Anna, Sister Angelina, Sister Agnes, and I received the habit. After we were vested, we returned with lighted candles, previously received at the altar. Four members also received the postulants' vesture. Sister Clara, Sister Frances, Sister Elizabeth, and Sister Mary had already donned their postulants' dress, so to complete their garb, they received the black bonnets. Usually Sisters invite their families for a religious celebration such as this, but we didn't invite anyone. There would have been no one to

---

58 The statue of Our Lady of Victory stood for many years in the Chapel of St. Joseph Home. A replica of it in fine white Italian Carrara marble is now in the foyer of the Motherhouse in Lemont.

serve them or us. We had to do everything ourselves. Consequently, we received our religious attire in the presence of our residents who cried from joy when we re-entered the chapel.

Father Andrew celebrated a Low Mass, during which we received Holy Communion and prayed fervently. There was nothing to distract our composure. After Holy Mass, Father intoned the Magnificat, and we sang it together with the greatest devotion, and without any previous rehearsals. And so concluded the ceremony of the first investiture in our Community.

In the afternoon we entertained some guests who came from curiosity to see whether we were vested and how we were dressed.[59] On the following day, Father Piechowski, pastor of St. Hedwig Parish, came with four Sisters of the Congregation of the Holy Family of Nazareth who taught in his school. He celebrated Holy Mass and then expressed his congratulations on the happiness that was ours that day. He also wished that our Community would develop and prosper. At breakfast, he mentioned that

---

59   The first habits of the Sisters very much resembled those of the School Sisters of Notre Dame. The reason for this is easily understood. Sisters of that order taught in St. Stanislaus Kostka Parish for a number of years. In the years since, the habit has necessarily undergone many modifications. The Sisters' garb today bears very little resemblance to the original worn by Mother Theresa.

he had a few candidates whom he intended to send to us. He also promised to help whenever possible. Later, his assistant, Father Gieburowski, came to see us. He became our confessor for a short time.

Accepting a crowd of orphans

Toward the end of May, our Father announced that we would have to accept orphans from the orphanage on Division Street. A year earlier, when the late Father Vincent mentioned to me that most likely we will also be getting orphans in our care, I became alarmed at this because I thought that we are still not well instructed in Religious life, nor are we aware of how a Religious should conduct herself. And here we are expected to rear and educate orphans. I told Father that if that had to be done, we would need more spiritual instruction and guidance in bringing them up properly. Father simply answered: "As God shall ordain." It was left at that, although I did not think that it would materialize so soon.

Joey, legless orphan

Now that Father told us that the orphans could no longer remain where they were because the building was to be converted into a high school, we knew definitely that we would have to take care of them. Another problem arose, therefore, since we did not have any room to house them. We decided to remodel the fourth floor in St. Joseph Home, in spite of the fact that it was the only place we used for doing our wash in the winter season. However, Father settled that problem by telling us to take the washing machines and dryers from the orphanage. In order to keep the cost at a minimum, we gave the carpentry work to Mr. Aloysius Krolikowski and a legless cripple Joseph, who was quite skillful with his hands. Plastering cost us somewhat more because we had to hire workmen. When the fourth floor was completed about the middle of July of 1899, Father Andrew brought twenty-four of the older orphan girls, but the younger girls and boys still remained in the orphanage.

These were placed in the charge of one of the Brothers of the Resurrectionist Order and also Father Kuszynski, who was then the Superior of the college, so titled, but later changed to high school. The Notre Dame Sisters, who till then provided for the orphans, left the orphanage on August 12, 1899. Before their departure, they brought twelve infants. Every space now in our home was occupied. The children, the old people, and the Sisters were all housed in that one building.

The Brother, left in charge of the boys at the orphanage, could not carry on with the 27 boys. Just two weeks after the Sisters left, we were called to the Brother's rescue. Father Andrew asked for two of our Sisters to take care of the boys at the orphanage until they could be moved to the new building that we would have to erect quickly, next to our original building.

Since we had no one available, we sent two candidates, the present Sister Clara and Sister Mary, to care for the boys. Our hands were full with all the work already placed on us, the four novices and four candidates. God, seeing our difficult circumstances, sent more candidates to our Community. On June 29, the present Sister Hedwig[60] entered and was later sent to the orphanage to help Sister Mary Clara, and Sister Mary returned to the Motherhouse. On the 5th of July, Sister Andrew[61] came from Holy Trinity Parish. Also, on August 2, Sister Kunegunda[62] entered from St. Hedwig Parish, while on August 12, Sister Veronica[63] was welcomed. And so our Community was increasing. On the 14th of August, two candidates entered, namely, Sister Aloysia[64] and Sister Rose.[65] We then had ten candidates

---

60 Sister Hedwig, former Rosalie Kubera, was born on September 6, 1878, and died on May 25, 1967.
61 Sister Mary Andrew, former Monica Zawadzka, was born on July 5, 1874, and died on August 15, 1929.
62 Sister Kunegunda, former Marianna Pinkowska, was born on December 18, 1880, and died on January 27, 1958.
63 Sister Veronica, former Louisa Maka, was born on May 7, 1865, and died on October 31, 1934.
64 Sister Aloysia, former Estelle Holysz, was born on October 26, 1879. She entered the community at the age of 20. A year after her Novitiate, she became a Superior of the branch house of Cragin. She was chosen Mother General of the Community in 1916. She died on March 18, 1955.
65 Sister M. Rose, former Maryann Gorska, was born on December 13, 1881, and died on July 2, 1959.

altogether. They were given to my charge for training. Also the admission of candidates was delegated to me.

Construction of St. Vincent Orphanage and new chapel

At the end of October, 1899, St. Vincent Home for the Orphans was started. Its construction proceeded quite rapidly, and twenty-seven boys were transferred from the orphanage on December 21. On Christmas Eve, which then fell on a Sunday, St. Vincent Home was blessed by the Reverend O.J. Kasprzycki, the pastor of St. Stanislaus Kostka Church. This dedication was rather a private one. Only Father Andrew and a few members of St. Stanislaus Parish attended this ceremony.

During the blessing of the chapel Father Kasprzycki delivered a sermon in which he also encouraged the Sisters to keep order and cleanliness in the chapel, extend due respect to this holy place, and influence others toward the same end—especially those who were placed under our care.

After the guests left, Father Andrew transferred the Blessed Sacrament from the old chapel to the new one. We set the various statues in their proper places so that the services could be celebrated on Christmas Day in the new chapel of St. Vincent Home.

The Christmas Midnight Mass was the first Mass offered in the new chapel. It was also the first time when a High Mass was celebrated in our home. Because of space limitations, there was no room for an organ in the old chapel. Our good Father procured one for us, but we still had no organist. The Midnight Mass was played by Mr. Kochanski, and his choir sang. It was something joyous for us, and especially for me, since my desire of last year had now been fulfilled. During the second Mass, Brother Adalbert, the organist of St. Hyacinth Church, played and the girls of the parish choir sang. For the first time we had benediction with the Blessed Sacrament exposed in a monstrance; thus far we had it reserved only in the ciborium. Everything seemed to be enlivened with all these festive additions.

Year 1900: Jubilee Year

The first of the New Year was most solemnly celebrated because the nineteenth century was ending. We had a Midnight Mass as at Christmas, and we all received Holy Communion. After Mass we sang the Te Deum.

As far as our domestic affairs were concerned, there were some changes. In September, 1899, the washing machines and dryers were moved from the orphanage to us. Then again we undertook doing the laundry for St. Stanislaus Kostka rectory and for those orphan boys who remained in the orphanage. The laundry was located where we at present had storage for provisions. It was much easier now to do the wash by machine instead of by hand.

Foundress (novice) burdened with innumerable duties

The administration of our Community had been placed in charge of the following: Sister Anna was the Superior; Sister Angeline, cashier, secretary, and sewing instructor. I was in charge of the candidates. The number had increased to fourteen towards the end of the 19th century; four ladies entered in November. On November 1, the present Sister Vincent[66] entered, and on the 21st, three more candidates were admitted namely: Barbara Reich,[67] Martha Grabowski,[68] and Philomena Suchomski.[69] They later obtained their religious names which were respectively, Sister Stanislaus, Sister Salomea, and Sister Josepha. I was also placed in charge of the aged residents, the laundry, mending and the distribution of all the washed articles, and the sewing of the clothes for the new candidates. Consequently, I had work in abundance to keep me constantly occupied.

---

66 Sister Vincent, former Maryann Czyzewska, was born on August 17, 1875, and died on April 22, 1942.
67 Barbara Reich, convent name Sister M. Stanislaus, was born on December 5, 1879, and died on April 27, 1958. She entered on November 21, 1899, and re-entered on November 29, 1910.
68 Martha Grabowska, convent name, Sister M. Salomea, was born July 3, 1879, and died at the Motherhouse in Lemont on February 13, 1969.
69 Philomena Suchomski, religious name Sister M. Josepha, was born on April 22, 1876, and died on August 29, 1918.

Sister Agnes[70] was placed in charge of the older orphan girls until the boys came. Later Sister Clara took over the girls, while Sister Frances, who was the cook, took care of the boys. The small children very often had a different Sister as Mother until the right one was found. On February 2, 1900, Sister Felixa[71] entered our Community; and on March 19, Sister Philipina.[72]

When Lent began, our solicitous Father Andrew purchased the Stations of the Cross for our chapel and invited a Franciscan Father from Polk Street to bless them on the First Friday of Lent.

First vows in the Community — June 3, 1900

While we were all so occupied with our work, the time of our Novitiate was fast coming to an end. I was not anxiously awaiting its completion because my inward desire was that we have another year's extension of this probation. I didn't know the opinion of the other Sisters, but I was of the belief that persons who want to bind themselves with religious vows ought to be better prepared and tried out, and not the way in which we spent our Novitiate. Each one did and said whatever she pleased, thus causing frequent misunderstandings, quarrels, and disturbances. The reason was that there were some among us who were not called to the Religious life, but they could not be dismissed according to the procedure of the other convents. Consequently, I was not overly anxious to make holy profession; but later my doubt disappeared after I placed myself entirely in submission to the Will of God.

> *My doubt disappeared after I placed myself entirely in submission to the Will of God.*

On the 28th of May, we started the retreat in preparation for taking our vows. There were four of us novices and eight postulants for the

---

70 Josephine Roszak, Sister M. Agnes, was born on November 30, 1864, entered on October 4, 1900, and died on April 7, 1931.
71 Stella Karwata, Sister M. Felixa, was born on October 30, 1880, entered on February 2, 1900, and died on April 24, 1920.
72 Cecelia Lama, Sister M. Philipina, was born on April 22, 1877, entered on March 19, 1900, and died on January 11, 1958.

Novitiate. Father Stephen Dabrowski was the retreat master. Toward the end of the retreat we felt that we were more strengthened spiritually. On Pentecost Sunday, which fell on June 3 that year, we pronounced the first vows in our Community during the Mass celebrated by Father Andrew. The ceremony[73] was more solemn than our reception to the Novitiate; but for me, there was more distraction because we still had no competent organist. Our Sisters did not yet know how to play the organ; therefore we asked Mr. Wiedemann from St. Hedwig Parish to play. Instead of coming himself, he sent a man who did not rehearse with the Sisters' choir. As could be expected under such conditions, they could not harmonize, and the effect was unnerving. I would never wish to hear another rendition like that one. In the afternoon for Benediction, and on the following day for the Mass, we had the assistance of Mr. Bubacz from St. Stanislaus College.

The second ceremony took place on the following day to welcome eight postulants to the Novitiate. They received the holy habit of our Congregation from the hands of the Very Reverend J. Kasprzycki and in the presence of Father Andrew. The solemnity of the day was celebrated with greater pomp and preparation than our first reception. The novices also invited their parents and relatives. It was, more or less, the same ceremony during which the novices are received today. Those Sisters, who had their names changed when they became members of the Third Order of St. Francis, kept their names; the others received new ones.

Mother becomes Novice Mistress

The novices were placed in my care. I held that office from June 4, 1900 to the end of July, 1909; then Sister Stanislaus took over. Later, Sister Kunegunda became the Mistress of Novices. And once again we began to perform our daily functions with renewed zeal, even though great difficulties seemingly increased after we pronounced our vows.

Spiritual sufferings of Mother Foundress

As I had mentioned before, not all of the members were called to Religious life with the pure intention of serving and loving God. Some,

---
73 The document of the first vows pronounced by Mother has been conserved.

having a selfish motive, proved to be a source of trials to others as they disturbed silence and peace and incited other Sisters to discontent. Most of this was directed against me on the grounds that I, not being a Superior, watched the observance of the Rule and interfered with everything that was going on. The Sisters who murmured were usually those for whom the yoke of practicing the Rule and the Religious life was too burdensome to undertake. We meet up with such Religious even to this day.

I became somewhat accustomed to their murmuring since I had borne it already for six years. In a way, those criticisms of my conduct were no small advantage for my pride. I would want to bear more as long as God would not be offended, and I would consider it even great happiness to be able to suffer for the greater glory of God and the good of this Community. If I saw that the happiness of a Religious depended on conniving in everything, and each one would wish to do as she pleases, then in that case I would not want to give any displeasure to anyone. It was not a pleasure for me to see and to hear the Sisters complaining; but I understood this matter and acted accordingly. If I had this position and were held responsible, I could not act otherwise and burden my conscience. At the time of this writing, however, the obligation does not rest on me any longer; I am peaceful, and I will care only for myself.[74]

Those criticisms of my conduct were no small advantage for my pride. I would want to bear more as long as God would not be offended, and I would consider it even great happiness to be able to suffer for the greater glory of God and the good of this Community.

Spiritual training of Sisters

Father J. Gieburowski, an assistant at St. Hedwig Church, was our confessor. He came regularly and usually had a conference

---

74 Mother wrote these words in obedience to her spiritual director, Father Andrew Spetz.

preceding the confessions. He and Father Andrew composed various morning and evening prayers for us. Once he came very early in the morning and said all the prayers aloud with us; he made the meditation in the same manner as we were accustomed to make it.

Slowly the feast of the Immaculate Conception was approaching, and on that day six postulants were to be received to the Novitiate. Our confessor, Father J. Gieburowski, conducted the retreat. He delivered the conferences and made the meditation after the conferences together with us. Usually he occupied a place in the last pew in order to observe how the Sisters conducted themselves during the meditation periods. At the end of the retreat, that is on the 8th of December, he celebrated Holy Mass and performed the ceremonies of investiture. Only Sister M. Clara disturbed him during Mass with her playing on the organ. Father understood, however, that the Sisters were not yet proficient in music.

Year 1901

Father Gieburowski[75] was unable to guide us much longer. In the last week of Lent he left for Europe, where he still remains and probably will never return. Father Andrew, our principal director, had to resume the duty of a confessor and spiritual guide until 1908. Father W. Rapacz became our confessor for a year and was then appointed as our extraordinary confessor. In the following year, Father Kowalczyk was replaced by Father Dembinski who was appointed as our confessor and catechist.

And so the term of the Novitiate for the eight novices was coming to a close. Again we started the retreat—the three of us for the renewal of our vows and the novices for making their profession. We began the retreat on June 1 and finished it on the 6th, on which day the Feast of Corpus Christi occurred that year. Now that we had more help, we were able to divide the work also among the novices who performed the most necessary tasks. This enabled us to devote more time to the spiritual exercises of the retreat. Father Siatka was our retreat master.

---

75   All priests mentioned by Mother are from the Congregation of the Resurrection.

First renewal of vows

Three of us renewed our vows, but the fourth one was forbidden to renew them because her conduct during the past year was unbecoming for a person aspiring to become a Religious. Sister Agnes, therefore, was dismissed.

First acceptance of parochial school

Shortly after the ceremonies of profession, the pastor of Sts. Peter and Paul Church of Spring Valley asked us to assume the responsibility of teaching in his school.[76] We accepted it, and the first group of Sisters set out on August 27, 1901. Sister Mary Kunegunda was the Superior of that first mission of our Community; Sister Mary Clara, a teacher; and Sister Mary, a cook. The latter, however, did not persevere. She yielded to a great temptation by taking enough money for a trip and, without the Superior's knowledge, left to join her mother in Chicago. She took off her religious garb, but she felt very unhappy. She was ashamed to meet people and wouldn't even go outdoors. When we were informed about it, Sister Superior sent a Sister to her in order to see how she was getting along. Sister Mary begged them with tears to accept her again. She was re-admitted after a few days, but as a postulant, and with the permission of the Archbishop she received the garb of a novice. She made the retreat with the other novices and was also permitted to renew her vows. Nevertheless, she[77] had to take the last place in the rank procedure of her group.

---

76 The acceptance of this first parochial school brings the Community in contact with its first commitment to education.
77 Sister Mary was 19 at this time. Mother M. Theresa wrote this chronicle in obedience to her spiritual director. Her very expression points out how well Mother understood that soul. Later Sister Mary worked as a teacher and twice became a Superior.

I am returning again to the affairs of our Community. The time for the reception of the candidates to the Novitiate was approaching. The day was set for the 27th of July, and it was preceded by a five-day retreat under the direction of Father S. Rogalski, C.R. At the end of the retreat he invested five candidates in the religious habit. So again there were eleven novices.

At that time the Sisters who had been in charge of the orphans had been changed. Sister Vincent was appointed to take care of the girls and Sister Felixa, of the little children. And so the daily routine continued on its course.

The time for the profession of the six novices had arrived. It was set for the 8th of December, but had to be postponed to the 15th on account of the absence of Father Andrew. He had been invited for the dedication of the new school at Spring Valley. After his return, he took care to arrange the retreat and the profession ceremonies; Father Joseph conducted the conferences.

During the following year nothing unusual happened in our Community. Except for the daily troubles and endeavors of the Sisters, the orphans, and the aged whose numbers had been steadily increasing, everything else went on at its normal pace.

Office of the Blessed Virgin Mary

In the same year, that is 1901, we received the Little Office. That was accomplished through Father Andrew's efforts in having it printed by the Polish Daily News Publishing Company. The printing was begun in July and completed in August. We received the Office for the first time on September 8, 1901. It seemed to us as if a new life was begun because up to that time we had been reciting the Tertiary prayers, that is, the twelve Our Fathers, Hail Marys, and the Apostles Creed; also the Hours of the Blessed Virgin. When we received the Office books and tried to recite it in common, it was rather difficult from the beginning, but in due time we became quite proficient.

> *We received the Office for the first time on September 8, 1901. It seemed to us as if a new life was begun...*

Year 1902

Slowly the time was nearing for the eight Sisters to renew their vows. It was to take place on June 6, but it was postponed until August 2 since all the Sisters were not at home. Another reason for the postponement was the inability to procure a priest to conduct another retreat. On August 2, the five novices were to make their first vows; and the Sisters, who were to renew their vows, joined the novices in making the retreat. It began on July 27 under the direction of Father Andrew, whose main topic during the conferences was the explanation of the Rules and Constitutions. This retreat was made by ten professed Sisters and five novices. One Sister, out of the class of eight, did not wish to renew her vows and shortly afterwards left the Community. It was Sister Frances T. After the reception of the five novices into profession, there were no novices until the following reception which took place on December 8. At this same time, a postulant, Anastasia S., left the Community because she felt that she had no vocation to the Religious life.

Second acceptance of parochial school

In the same year, we accepted a new mission in Cragin, IL. The following Sisters were the pioneers: Sister Mary Aloysia, Superior; Sister Mary Philipina, teacher of English; and Sister Mary Gertrude, cook. They left for the new mission on August 26, 1902.

On the 4th of December, four postulants began a retreat in preparation for their Novitiate. A few other professed Sisters also participated in the same retreat, together with the six Sisters who made their first profession the previous year on December 15. They renewed their vows that year on December 8, 1902.

Year 1903

Purchase of two small houses and five lots in Avondale

Two houses and five lots were purchased on Ridgeway Avenue after the New Year. One house was situated where our present workroom is located. That house was blessed on the feast of St. Joseph and was named St. Theresa Home. The other was the one in which the aged now live, and it was named St. Joachim Home. It was blessed a little earlier than the former one.

In St. Joachim Home, we accommodated the Sisters from Spring Valley where a contagious disease raged. Since the school was closed, and the Sisters could not conduct any classes, they were obliged to return home. They were not allowed to enter the convent, but had to remain for some time in the small building. Since this occurred in February, and the winter was quite severe, they had to suffer on account of the cold, shortage of covers, and insufficient heating. When it became evident that there was no danger of communicating the disease, the Sisters were then allowed to come to the main building.

Influx of vocations

We placed the novices and postulants in the other house, leaving more room in the main building for the professed Sisters. Soon, however, both houses were filled to capacity—one, with the aged, and the other, with the ever-increasing number of postulants.

Now we wanted to buy the third house, but the proprietor would not sell it for the price we thought it was worth; but finally an agreement was made. We also purchased the two lots adjacent to that house, and then our property increased considerably. There were still those two last houses and lots, the last two in our half block; but because of the lack of money, we had no means to purchase them.

Providential mystery gift

After some time, God sent us a benefactor who, to this day, remains unknown. One day a certain man brought a world globe, which we have at present in the postulants' classroom. To it was attached a box containing $1,000. Since Sister Superior wished to purchase the two last houses, the property was soon obtained in agreement with the contents of the note which stated that the money should be used for our home. It was the Hand of Providence helping us. Not long after, Sister Superior found a little box on the table which contained another $1,000. The note stated that the money was given at the Community's disposal.

After the disease was checked, the Sisters returned to Spring Valley around Easter. Sister Salomea was sent in place of Sister Seraphine,[78] who remained at home. Nevertheless, shortly after the Sisters' arrival in Spring Valley, the pastor left the parish without arranging for a substitute. The Sisters kept teaching school till vacation and attended the distant Lithuanian church, which made it very inconvenient. When vacation came, the Sisters returned home permanently.

Acceptance of third parochial school

In place of that mission, another school was accepted in Cleveland, OH. The Sisters left for the new mission on October 18, 1903. They were Sister Mary Clara as Superior, Sister Mary Seraphine, Sister Mary Agnes, and a postulant, Sister Mary Bonaventure.[79]

First 40 Hour Devotions in Community chapel

On October 4 of the same year, six postulants were received to the Novitiate. There were again ten novices until December 8, and on that day four of them were admitted to profession. On December 10 of that year,

---

78 Martha Zamrowski, Sister M. Seraphine, entered on July 2, 1900 and died on September 7, 1949.
79 Frances Blazek, Sister M. Bonaventure, entered on February 2, 1903 and died on November 10, 1912.

through the efforts of Father Andrew, we held Forty Hours Devotion for the first time.

Portiuncula indulgence[80] for Community chapel

In the previous year, that is on August 2, 1902, we received the privilege to gain the Portiuncula indulgence in our chapel. Although our little chapel was small and poor, it had been enriched with this indulgence.

Year 1904

First convent infirmary

The year 1904 arrived. Nothing extraordinary happened in our daily routine at the beginning of that year. The third house, which I had mentioned before, was converted into an infirmary, and at the blessing, it received the name of St. Ann Hospital. After the last two houses were somewhat remodeled, the postulants lived in one of them for a short time, while the other one housed aged women.

Mother Anne's illness

In June, our Sister Superior took sick and this saddened us all. I had difficulty in managing everything since I had to take over her duties. I also had to take care of the postulants, novices and, at that time, even the professed Sisters. This continued for almost two months, during which time Sister Superior was recuperating in our St. Ann Infirmary. When she recovered, she resumed her responsibilities.

---

80 See Appendix for information about how St. Francis asked for and obtained the Indulgence of Forgiveness.

First visit of Archbishop of Chicago

Toward the end of July, we received the first canonical visitation made personally by the Most Reverend Archbishop James Edward Quigley.[81] He had been just recently installed in the diocese and was making visits to each parish and institution under his jurisdiction. So he also came to us. The orphans greeted him with songs and speeches in the dining room. After the welcoming program, Archbishop Quigley proceeded to the chapel and imparted his blessing to the assembled old people. He then went to observe almost every room in the orphanage, some of the rooms of the aged, the kitchen and the dining room. Lastly, he visited the infirmary where Sister Superior had been recuperating; she never expected him to visit her. He spoke with her and asked questions about some matters relating to the Community. After lunch the Archbishop left us and promised to see us at the next visitation, six years hence.

When vacation time was approaching, all of our Sisters from the missions returned to make their retreat. In that year, the Sisters came from two missions. The retreat had been divided into two sessions. The first one began on July 22, and the other took place at the end of September.

Blessed Kunegunda as patroness of Community

In the first retreat, nine postulants participated in preparation for their Novitiate; the ceremony took place on July 27, the feast of Blessed

---

[81] Archbishop Quigley was the Archbishop of Chicago from 1902 to 1915.

Kunegunda, the patroness[82] of our Community. Prior to taking their vows, six novices took part in the September retreat.

Embrace of St. Elizabeth Nursery

At this time we accepted the Day Nursery on Ashland and Blackhawk Streets in Chicago.[83] Sister Mary Angelina went there as Superior, accompanied by Sister Mary Clara and Sister Mary Hyacinth.[84] Sister Mary Felix was sent there later. The Sisters started their work in the nursery at the beginning of August. Their duties were to take care of the pre-school-age children whose mothers were forced to work in order to support their families. The Sisters also taught catechism to the children who could not attend parish schools and prepared them for their First Holy Communion.

Fourth parochial school accepted

In the same year we also accepted a mission in Berlin, WI. On September 18, our Sisters went there to teach in the local school. Sister Mary Rose was sent as Superior; Sister Mary Salomea and Sister Mary Frances as teachers; and Sister Mary Louise, the newly professed, was sent there as a cook on the 6th of October.

---

82 In the year 1892, the 600th anniversary of the death of Blessed Kunegunda was celebrated. At this time action for her canonization began. Every parish conducted by the Resurrection Fathers became involved in the festivities. Seemingly, then, at her own conviction and the urging of Father Barzynski, Mother Theresa adopted Blessed Kunegunda as patroness. The photograph shows an iconic style image of St. Kunegunda near a vessel of salt topped by wedding bands. Legend tells of St. Kunegunda tossing her ring into a stream which later revealed a huge deposit of salt, an invaluable commodity in medieval Poland. Kunegunda was canonized in 1999 by Pope John Paul II.
83 Not mentioned by Mother is a non-resident medical nursery also staffed by the Sisters and several volunteer physicians.
84 Miss Barczewski, Sister M. Hyacinth, entered on October 3, 1902 and died on November 5, 1972.

Death of Agnes Dudzik, Mother of Mother Theresa

After a brief illness my beloved mother[85] died on October 26, and she was buried on the 28th.

Later, nothing extraordinary happened outside of the constant increase of new vocations and our Community continuing to grow rapidly. On the 13th of November, two Sisters of the Holy Family of Nazareth left their Community and, with the consent of Father Andrew, were admitted into ours. They were Sister Michael[86] and Sister Augustine.[87] However, since they did not have the dispensation from the Holy See from their vows, which they took in the other community, they were not allowed to enter the candidacy. They were not immediately accepted to the postulancy, but had to undergo a few months of probation as aspirants. The postulant bonnet was given to them on the feast of St. Joseph in 1905. Sister Michael spent 18 years in the Holy Family of Nazareth Order, and Sister Augustine, 11 years. Both had made their perpetual vows, but they received dispensation on the day preceding their reception into the Novitiate on November 28, 1905.

---

85 Agnes Dudzik, nee Polaszczyk, the mother of Mother Theresa, came to the United States in 1881. She was admitted to St. Joseph Home for the Aged on December 22, 1894. The official death records show the date of October 24, although Mother Theresa has October 26 as the day. Mrs. Dudzik's funeral took place in St. Joseph's chapel and she is buried next to her husband in St. Adalbert cemetery (Death certificate of Mother Theresa's Father, John, shows his death as May 12, 1889. Her sister, Marianne died in 1878.
86 Apolonia Sobieszczyk, Sister M. Michael, entered on November 13, 1904 and died on October 15, 1935.
87 Anna Malinowski, Sister M. Augustine, entered on November 13, 1904 and died on August 3, 1942.

Year 1905

In January, 1905, Sister Aloysia, who had been a Superior in Cragin, became sick and had to return to the Motherhouse. She was replaced by Sister Philipina as the Superior, while Sister Susan and Sister Mary helped in teaching. Sister Aloysia recovered after convalescing several months.

New house, Novitiate, and laundry

I also wish to mention that at the beginning of October, 1904, a new building had been started for the Novitiate and laundry.

New laundry upgraded

In January, 1905, the washing machines were transferred from the old laundry to the new one, and additional laundry equipment was purchased. It was so much easier for me then, for I had great difficulties due to the unsuitable place in which the machines were located. Because of insufficient room, the novices and the candidates were transferred to the second floor.

When vacation time came, the retreat had to be divided into three series. The Sisters arrived home from four of our missions for retreat and some for the renewal of their vows. On July 21, the first series began for the six postulants who were to be received to the Novitiate on July 26. The second series began in August for the nine novices who were to make their profession; and, lastly, fifteen professed Sisters began their retreat for the renewal of their vows. Eleven of these Sisters renewed their vows for a period of five years. This ceremony took place on the feast of St. Clare, August 12.

Archbishop Simon, papal delegate of Pius X

Toward the end of July of that year we had the honor of having with us a distinguished guest from Europe. It was His Excellency, Archbishop

Simon,[88] who had been visiting that year almost all the Polish churches and institutions in the United States. He was greeted by the orphans in the refectory, and then came to the chapel where the Sisters and the aged were gathered. The Archbishop delivered a short sermon and imparted his blessing. He departed after we all kissed his ring.

First vocations from Cleveland, OH

I wish to mention that when our Sisters returned home from Cleveland for their vacation, they came along with two postulants. One of them was Sister Ignatia,[89] and the other one was dismissed because of her mental condition after a year of probation.

On August 17, 1905, our Sisters left for their assigned posts at various missions. There were some changes made, and on that day, Sister Mary Stanislaus, Sister Mary Seraphine, and Sister Mary Leona[90] were sent to teach; and Sister Mary Agnes and a postulant went to perform domestic work.

During that same month Sister Mary Salomea,[91] Sister Mary Hugoline, and Sister Mary Philomena[92] went to Berlin, WI to teach; and Sister Mary Hyacinth and a postulant were sent to do kitchen duties. Sister Mary Angeline, Sister Mary Clara, Sister Mary Felixa and two postulants were sent to the Day Nursery.

Sister Mary Philipina, Sister Mary and Sister Mary Susan went to Cragin to teach; and Sister Mary Cajetan[93] and Rosalie, a postulant, were commissioned to do domestic work.

---

88   Archbishop was a papal delegate.
89   Anastasia Dukowski, Sister M. Ignatia, entered on July 16, 1905 and died on July 6, 1911.
90   Bernice Pochelski, Sister M. Leona, entered on September 17, 1901 and died on October 23, 1954.
91   Sister M. Salomea, the former Martha Grabowski, was born on July 3, 1879, and died on February 13, 1969.
92   Anna Marszalkowski, Sister M. Philomena, entered on November 30, 1903 and died on August 6, 1914.
93   Sophie Tabasz, Sister M. Cajetan, entered on August 2, 1903 and died on June 10, 1953.

Fifth and sixth schools accepted by Community

In that year, we accepted two more missions. One was in Oshkosh, WI, and the other one was St. Casimir School in St. Louis, MO, where Father Gnielinski was pastor. The Sisters left for St. Louis, MO on September 9. Sister Mary Aloysia went as a Superior; Sister Mary Frances, Sister Mary Dominic,[94] Sister Mary Jolanta,[95] and two postulants went to teach; Sister Mary Barbara[96] was sent to do domestic work and, a little later, Sophie, a postulant, was sent to help in the kitchen.

Shortly after the Sisters arrived on that mission, the pastor left the parish secretly, went to Europe and never returned. This caused a great deal of unpleasantness for the Sisters and even aroused a disturbance among the parishioners. This I would not be able to describe, because I do not remember all the unpleasant happenings.

On September 13, Sister Mary Gerarda[97] was appointed Superior to Oshkosh; one postulant went to teach, and Sister Mary Patricia[98] was sent to do the kitchen duties. In about the middle of November, Sister Mary Patricia was recalled to the Motherhouse because of her disobedience, and a postulant, Rosalie K., replaced her in the kitchen. Sister Mary Colette[99] also accompanied the postulant since she was to do substitute work in the classroom for Sister Mary Gerarda, the Superior. She became ill and needed eye surgery. After she recovered, Sister Mary Colette returned to the Motherhouse. Shortly afterwards, however, the postulant who had been working there in the kitchen also had to be recalled home on account of disobedience; and Sister Mary Jolanta took over the kitchen tasks. That postulant was dismissed from our Community on March 30.

---

94 Rosalie Makowski, Sister M. Dominic, entered on December 7, 1902 and died on February 10, 1937.
95 Joanna Nowak, Sister M. Jolanta, entered on March 19, 1903 and died on August 17, 1970.
96 Mary Grochola, Sister M. Barbara, entered on August 2, 1903 and died on May 11, 1961.
97 Mary Gorzkowski, Sister M. Gerarda, entered on May 27, 1903 and died on February 2, 1964.
98 Lauretta Eiress, Sister M. Patricia, entered on July 26, 1903 and died on September 29, 1959.
99 Frances Nowak, Sister M. Colette, entered on May 17, 1901 and died on September 25, 1945.

Change of Superiors

On October 4 of the same year, the Superior of the Motherhouse was changed. Venerable Sister Mary Anna was the Superior for seven years. Now Sister Mary Vincent had been appointed for this position by our spiritual director, Father Andrew. Sister Mary Vincent[100] was in charge of the orphan girls for several years.

Mother M. Theresa, assistant

A month later, I was appointed as her first assistant and also as mistress of novices and postulants; Sister Mary Angeline had been appointed second councilor; Sister Mary Rose, third councilor and secretary of the council. She was also a portress and had to settle all the business affairs. She held her positions only for several months since she was unable to fulfill her duties because of illness.

Sister M. Antonina, first nurse in Community

On October 12, Sister Mary Bonaventure went to New Mexico to St. Joseph Sanitarium to regain her health. She remained there for almost a year. About the 20th of the same month, Sister Mary Antonina[101] and Frances,[102] a postulant, went to Lafayette, IN to the hospital of the Franciscan Sisters for a course in hospital training. Sister Mary Antonina was to learn the procedure of nursing the sick, in which she already had a few months of training at Mercy Hospital in Chicago, and the postulant was to obtain some pharmaceutical knowledge.

After the middle of November, Mary, the postulant, returned from St. Louis to prepare for her reception into the Novitiate. Sister Mary, who was in Cragin, was recalled home because of illness. She had

---

100 Sister M. Vincent was born in 1875. She entered the Community in 1899. In 1905 she became Superior of the Community and in 1922 she became Mother General. She died on April 22, 1942.
101 Catherine Osinski, Sister M. Antonine, entered on November 13, 1902. She was elected Superior General in 1934 and died on May 4, 1963.
102 Frances Jakaitis, Sister M. Benigna, entered on October 4, 1905 and died on March 16, 1970.

been replaced by Cecilia, a postulant. After regaining her health, Sister Mary was sent to St. Louis. During the Christmas holidays Sister Mary Aloysia and Sister Mary Frances came to the Motherhouse to ask for a better teacher. Since we had no other competent one available, we sent a novice, Sister Mary Chester,[103] while Sister Mary Jolanta, who had some scholastic difficulties, returned to the Motherhouse on January 3.

November 23 marked the beginning of a retreat for the 13 postulants in preparation for their Novitiate. They received the religious habit on the 29th, the feast of All Saints of the Orders of Our Father St. Francis. There were nineteen novices at that time.

Year 1906

Building of historic greenhouse

The year 1906 arrived. It began in the usual manner, with no extraordinary happenings except for the few changes of Sisters which I mentioned above.

Twenty-nine novices

That summer the Sisters returned to the Motherhouse from six missions. The retreat again had to be divided into three series. The first began on July 21 for the ten postulants who were preparing for their reception into the Novitiate. Twenty-one professed Sisters also took part in that retreat. On the 26th of July, these ten postulants received the religious habit, increasing the number of novices to twenty-nine until August 15. On the following day, that is July 27, the feast of the Patroness of our Congregation was celebrated. The second retreat began on August 10 for the six novices in preparation for profession and for the nine professed Sisters, whose renewal of temporary vows was to take place on August 15.

---

103 Martha Dziarnowski, Sister M. Chester, entered on October 3, 1904 and died on January 19, 1963.

Seventh school accepted

After the feast of the Assumption, the Sisters left for their assigned missions. At the same time, the transfer of Sisters took place. With the end of the school year, we closed St. Casimir School in East St. Louis, MO. This was due to the poor attitude of the parishioners toward the new pastor and because of the shortage of Sisters for teaching. Instead, we accepted St Stanislaus Kostka School in the same city.

Sister Mary Colette went to this school as a Superior in August; Sister Mary Bonaventure went there directly from the sanatorium in New Mexico; Sister Mary Zita[104] and Sister Mary Brigid[105] went to teach; and Sister Mary Barbara and Magdalene, a postulant, went to perform domestic work.

After the departure of our Sisters to the various missions, Father Andrew left for California where he spent three weeks visiting the mines.

First serious illness of Mother Theresa

On October 21, 1906, I became ill and therefore do not remember accurately anything of great importance to note except that on December 8 of that year thirteen novices made their temporary vows; and twelve postulants were received into the Novitiate on the same day. During my illness of more than six months, Sister Mary Hedwig was in charge of the novices, while Sister Mary Vincent, the Superior, took care of the postulants and the aged. When I recovered, I took over the novices only. Due to my physical weakness, the postulants and the aged had been given to the care of another Sister.

---

104   Frances Kosmala, Sister M. Zita, entered on February 2, 1904 and died on December 31, 1974.
105   Victoria Czuj, Sister M. Brigid, entered on September 8, 1904 and died on January 28, 1971.

Year 1907

Mother undergoes surgery

I also remember that Sister Mary Antonina returned to Lafayette for training after vacation, while the postulant who had been with her the previous year, went into the Novitiate. Sister Mary Antonina contracted typhoid fever and was sick for over two months. She was so weak that she was unable to study anymore or perform any hard work. She was ordered to return to the Motherhouse at the end of November and then was sent for recuperation to Berlin, WI. After regaining her strength, she returned to the Motherhouse in May, 1907. Since then she never returned to finish her training. Instead, he took charge of our infirmary at the Motherhouse and continued studying hospital work privately.

In 1907, the Sisters returned, as usual, to the Motherhouse for the vacation period. After making the retreat, nine novices were admitted to their First Profession on July 27; Sister Mary W. was suspended from the Community on the 8th of December. Twelve postulants were admitted to the Novitiate on August 15.

Eighth school accepted

During that vacation we accepted another mission in Indiana Harbor. We changed the mission from Berlin, WI to East St. Louis, IL because of the lack of funds for the maintenance of teachers in Berlin. On the 7th of September, the Sisters left the Motherhouse for East St. Louis, and in the meantime their belongings were moved from Berlin to East St. Louis. Sister Mary Salomea was sent as a Superior, Sister Mary Hugoline to teach, and Sister Mary Leocadia[106] was sent to do domestic work. On September 21, Sister Mary Kunegunda went to Indiana Harbor as a Superior, and with her went Sister Mary Stephanie and Sister Mary Jolanta, but the latter remained there only until October 6 because of various difficulties she encountered.

---

106 Antoinette Das, Sister M. Leocadia, entered on October 3, 1904 and died on August 23, 1960

She was replaced by Sister Mary Theophilia.[107] A little later, Sister Mary Veronica was sent there to recuperate from her previous surgery.

Mother Theresa's second surgery

On November 13, I suffered a relapse and was re-admitted to the hospital.[108] Being quite weak then, I did not recall very well the events which occurred at that time except that I possessed a note which describes the festival of December 8, the feast of the Immaculate Conception of the Blessed Virgin Mary. On that day, fourteen professed Sisters renewed their temporary vows during the Mass which was celebrated by Father Andrew. He also delivered an inspiring sermon for the occasion. The next festive day was on the 10th of December when thirteen novices made their first vows. The ceremony was performed by Father Andrew, and the Mass was celebrated by Father Filipski who, after the ceremony, delivered a sermon about the solemnity of that moment. He also gave the Benediction with the Blessed Sacrament.

Statue of Blessed Kunegunda

A statue of Blessed Kunegunda was blessed by the Resurrectionist Fathers on Sunday, December 15, at three o'clock in the afternoon. After the ceremonial blessing of the statue, Father W. Zapala, C.R. delivered a dedication talk.

On December 19, 20, and 21, a Forty Hours Devotion was held in our chapel, which was crowded with guests. The devotions were announced in the Polish Daily News and guests had been invited to attend the Forty Hours Adoration.

Year 1908

The year 1908 arrived. Nothing unusual occurred. The first event to be noted was that three of our Sisters departed to Lafayette for

---

107   Sophie Stasiek, Sister M. Theophila, entered on September 8, 1905 and died on January 26, 1951.
108   Mother was re-admitted on November 7th and had surgery on the 12th.

nurses training in January. Sister Mary Benigna, the former postulant Frances Jakaitis, who had been taking pharmaceutical instructions, returned to continue her studies as a pharmacist. She finished the required course in five months, and then continued at the College of Medicine every other day for two years. Sister Mary Ladislaus[109] and Sister Mary Dionisia were in training for three years and then received their diplomas as registered nurses.

Bishop's visit — Confirmations

In June of the same year we had a guest, the Most Reverend Archbishop Moldoon, who came to visit our institution and to confirm some of our orphans. One novice was confirmed and a few ladies of St. Elizabeth Society. Many members of that society gathered in our home for that occasion plus a number of neighboring priests attended the ceremony and then remained for dinner.

First daily Mass offered in chapel

In the same month, we obtained a resident chaplain in the person of the late Father Victor Rodowicz,[110] a 70-year-old priest. Although the Holy Sacrifice of the Mass was our greatest desire, it was only celebrated on Sundays, holydays of obligation, during retreat, and on some special occasions. Despite the fact that the chaplain was elderly and infirm, very forgetful, and at times made mistakes when he celebrated the Holy Sacrifice of the Mass, it was a pleasure for us because we were able to receive Holy Communion often.

---

109 Mary Wroblewski, Sister M. Ladislaus, entered on December 7, 1904 and died on March 20, 1965.
110 Father Victor Rodowicz was a retired priest unable to do parish work.

Death of first Sister in Community

On the 30th of July of that same year, Sister Mary Delphine[111] died, the first Sister of our Community. Her maiden name was Anna Miszewski, and she was born in Western Prussia, Europe. She died of tuberculosis at the age of twenty-seven, after three years of illness. Her funeral took place on August 1, a time during which most of the Sisters were able to attend the services. After the Office of the Dead had been recited, our spiritual director, Father Andrew, celebrated the Mass; Father S. Swierczek, the assistant of St. Hyacinth Church, delivered the eulogy. The body was escorted to its final resting place in St. Adalbert Cemetery by the priests of the Resurrectionist Order, our Sisters, and a few Sisters of other Communities. It was laid in the first grave of the section recently reserved for the burial of the Sisters of our Congregation. May she rest in peace!

All the Sisters from the various missions could not be accommodated for the annual retreat because of the lack of space. They were, therefore, divided into two groups. The first retreat took place before July 27, and the second started on August 9 under the direction of Father Ladom, who prepared thirteen novices for their first profession and some professed Sisters for the renewal of their temporary vows on August 15. Although some changes had been made, the rest of the Sisters returned to their respective missions after the retreats and ceremonies.

Ninth school accepted

We again accepted a new mission in Hegewisch that year, in spite of the fact that we did not have enough teachers. But because of the pleading of the pastor, and trusting in God that He is calling us there to help this priest, we were confident that He would also help us in these difficulties. On September 21, 1908, the Sisters left for that mission to take care of the school children. Sister Mary Colette went as Superior; Sister Mary Chester,

---

111 Anna Miszewski, Sister M. Delphine, entered on July 13, 1903, and died on July 30, 1908.

Sister Mary Boniface,[112] and a postulant were teachers; and Sister Mary Barbara was sent to perform domestic duties. After that event, nothing worthy of notice happened until the following New Year.

Year 1909

Mother Theresa again General Superior of Community

The year 1909 brought us more worries and trouble. On the 1st of January, Sister Mary Vincent, the Superior General who held the office for three years and three months, had been changed and replaced by me (Sister Mary Theresa)[113] who had been the mistress of novices. Sister Mary Hedwig was appointed first councilor; Sister Mary Angeline, the second councilor; Sister Mary Aloysia, the third councilor and secretary of the council; and Sister Mary Vincent was made procurator.

Spiritual renewal of the Community

From that time we began, as our Rule directed, regular monthly assemblies for the discussion of Community problems. The Administrative Board began working especially on the revision of the rules which lacked clarity and detail. Father Andrew had noticed this and tried with great effort and our advice to compile a more understandable Rule. It would prove of great importance and necessity for the Administrative Board and every Sister to know her obligations, regardless of the office she holds or the duty she performs.

---

112   Magdalene Pranko, Sister M. Boniface, entered on December 7, 1905 and died on July 5, 1989.
113   On January 1, 1909, Father Spetz appointed Mother Theresa for this post. At the same time he left her as mistress of novices.

A copy of the revised Rule[114] was sent to the Most Reverend Archbishop Quigley who approved it and returned it to us. Copies were then distributed to all the Sisters at the various missions. The Rule was to be examined and practiced for a year, and every Sister was to decide whether it was suitable for our observance. At the first General Chapter, a report was to be given as to what practices were to be retained for permanent use and what was to be rejected.

Father Andrew's Silver Jubilee of Priesthood

Toward the end of April, our Father Director became ill and was confined to rest for some time. He was to celebrate his Silver Jubilee of priesthood on May 4 of that year. It would be a great festival for us, too, although we feared that he would be unable to celebrate Mass because of sickness. However, God permitted him to recover sufficiently; on the day preceding his jubilee feast, he left our home where he stayed during his illness. On the 4th of May, he celebrated his Solemn Jubilee Mass at St. Stanislaus Kostka Church, assisted by his brother[115] and two nephew-priests. This gave him the greatest joy since it is unusual to have so many priests from one family at the altar. Many priests from his Order and also many relatives and friends came from various places. Our three little orphans, dressed in white and adorned with wreaths on their heads, led Father Andrew to the altar. One of these little girls wore a veil and carried a cushion with a silver wreath, which she handed to Father Andrew at the altar.

Father Andrew's illness and his return to Europe thwarted plans for reform

Physical weakness had not abandoned Father Andrew completely. On the advice of his physician to take an ocean voyage, Father left for Europe in the middle of June and remained there for three months. His absence affected us greatly, and mainly me, because of the many plans that had been arranged for the summer months and because Father was also directing the construction of the second floor above the laundry.

---

114   A printed copy of these Constitutions is kept in the archives. It is an important document, representing the spirit of Mother.
115   The Resurrectionist Father Theobald Spetz is the mentioned brother.

Postponement of First General Chapter to 1910

Vacation was approaching. The retreat series had to be arranged, and Father Andrew was the sole director in this regard. Perpetual vows, which were to be taken for the first time in our Community, were postponed to December 8, and the General Chapter was postponed to the following year. Father S. Rogalski[116] substituted for Father Andrew in solving our minor problems. He obtained retreat masters for us and carried out the canonical examination for investiture and profession. God helped Father Andrew and us. He returned at the beginning of September, though not as strong as we had expected him to be. The first retreat began on July 9, during which six postulants prepared for their reception to the Novitiate on the 15th of July; the six novices made their profession on the 17th. A majority of the Sisters joined in this retreat, while the rest, and those for the renewal of their temporary vows, participated in the following retreat which began on August 9.

I also mention that on the 2nd of August of that year Sister Stanislaus, formerly Barbara Reich, left the Community secretly and went to her parents' home. She divested herself of her religious garb and returned to Cleveland to the parish where she was the former Superior for five years. Her reasons for leaving were evident. She did not want to remain in the Motherhouse where she was appointed as Mistress of Novices. She felt an aversion to this position; and when she noticed that her various petitions and recommendations would not be considered, and that she would not return to the same mission, she left the Motherhouse and went to Cleveland to stay at the rectory. We experienced a great deal of unpleasantness on account of her action. And until now we feel sorry for her because she had fallen low, and it was difficult for her to rise.

---

116 Reverend S. Rogalski was the Superior of St. Stanislaus Kostka Parish.

Tenth and eleventh schools accepted

After all the festivities and exercises had been finished, the Sisters again departed for their various missions. Many changes were made. We accepted two new missions—in Youngstown, OH, and Gary, IN.

Sister Mary Casimir[117] was sent to Youngstown on September 1 as a Superior, and she was accompanied by Sister Mary Seraphine, Sister Mary Salesia,[118] and a postulant. The last two were appointed to perform domestic duties. After the student enrollment was over, however, it was necessary to open three classrooms instead of two. Sister Mary Salesia was assigned to teach. Sister Mary Brigid was also sent there later.

The Sisters left for Gary, IN, on September 2. Sister Mary Jerome[119] was appointed Superior; Sister Mary and two postulants were also sent there—one to teach and the other one to perform domestic tasks.

I also want to point out that our Sisters were organists and directed choirs in the parishes of the following places: St. Louis, East St. Louis, Oshkosh, Whiting, Indiana Harbor, Hegewisch, and Gary.

Death of elderly chaplain

On October 17, our elderly chaplain, Fr. Victor Rodowicz, died after being ill for less than a week. The funeral was held at St. Hyacinth Church on October 19, and his body was laid to rest in St. Adalbert Cemetery in one of the lots belonging to us and reserved for the aged and the crippled. His bequests, amounting to $2,500, were transferred to us by Father Andrew who was appointed as the executor of the will.

---

117 Mary Janowiak, Sister M. Casimir, entered on October 29, 1904 and died on June 28, 1947.
118 Kathryn Rzeszutko, Sister M. Salesia, entered on February 2, 1907 and died on February 1, 1937.
119 Anna Dadej, Sister M. Jerome, entered on February 2, 1906. She was elected Superior General in 1946, re-elected in 1952, and died on November 1, 1970.

Mother Theresa's perpetual vows

Finally the time arrived to make our perpetual vows. We began the retreat on the 1st of December. The conferences were given by Father Siara. There were ten Sisters for perpetual vows and also some Sisters for the renewal of their temporary vows.

On the day of the religious ceremony, the first Mass was celebrated by our spiritual director, Father Andrew. During that Mass over twenty Sisters renewed their temporary vows. The second Mass was celebrated pontifically by the Most Reverend Bishop P. P. Rhode, who was assisted by Father Andrew and Father Dembinski. During the Mass we made our perpetual vows for the first time in our Congregation and also for the first time at the hands of a bishop. That was an extraordinary blessing. Before we pronounced our vows, the Bishop delivered an inspiring sermon about the meaning of the vows and our obligations. After the Mass he handed to each of us a little wooden crucifix, which we now wear on our bosom, and placed a wreath of thorns on each head. After the Benediction of the Blessed Sacrament, the Bishop confirmed two postulants. One was the bishop's relative, Mary Kirschbaum,[120] the other was Mary Narozna[121] from Texas.

On the day following the feast of the Immaculate Conception, Father Andrew became so ill that he was unable to have Mass for several days; his health gradually improved after a brief rest. Since that day, however, Father Andrew stayed with us permanently; he advised and guided not only the Sisters, but also the lay people who came to him for solutions to their problems and troubles.

I also include that on the third day after the funeral of our late chaplain we obtained another priest in his place. He was the Reverend Luke Swiatkowski, who remained with us until the end of January, 1910. He then moved to St. Stanislaus Kostka rectory.

---

120 Mary Kirschbaum, Sister M. Paul, entered on November 21, 1909 and died on March 13, 1961.
121 Mary Narozna, Sister M. Bernardine, entered on August 15, 1909 and died on January 24, 1912.

Year 1910

"I began preparations for the First Chapter"

On March 19, I was ordered by Father Andrew to prepare a tentative agenda and have it presented at the First General Chapter of our Congregation.

We had received a donation of three lots, valued at $1,000, from Mrs. Suwalski who had left that provision in her will.

In the same year, Mrs. H. Hanley of St. Joseph, Michigan, bequeathed us an acre of land containing an orchard of fruit trees and a berry path, together with a two-story building amounting to a total value of $1,000. During vacation time, prior to their arrival from various missions for the retreat, our Sisters spent a few weeks there and enjoyed the fresh air and rest. Some Sisters relaxed and studied in preparation for future work.

Twelfth school accepted

In that year we again accepted the mission in Spring Valley, where our Sisters had been teaching formerly.

The Sisters were returning to the Motherhouse from eleven missions at the beginning of the vacation period. Two series of retreats had been arranged. The first began on the 9th of July, during which five novices prepared themselves for profession, twenty-three postulants for their reception into the Novitiate, and thirty other professed Sisters participated in the spiritual exercises. The retreat master was Father Tudyka, who gave three conferences daily. The religious ceremonies took place on the 15th and the 16th of July.

On the 27th of the same month, on the feast of Blessed Kunegunda, the patroness of our Community, nine Sisters renewed their temporary vows for a period of two years.

Recollections for Sister delegates to the First Chapter

Another retreat began on the 3rd of August for the Sisters who were to take their vows on the feast of St. Clare, August 12. The delegates for the First General Chapter of our Congregation also participated in the last retreat. Altogether there were sixty Sisters who made the retreat, the largest number that we ever had for one series. The retreat master was Father Saborosz who, on August 12, celebrated the Mass and officiated at the ceremonies for receiving the perpetual vows. He delivered an inspiring sermon prior to the moment when the seven Sisters pledged themselves to observe their perpetual vows.

CONCLUSION OF MANUSCRIPT

I am now closing this chronicle of our Community.[122] It contains many deficiencies[123] and inadequacies because I cannot recall all the happenings. I did not have the opportunity to write down all the various minor occurrences from the beginning of our Community. The more important ones I have written down, inasmuch as I remember them. Now I beg you to forgive me for all the inaccuracies and my terrible handwriting. I believe that the Sisters are aware of my lack of higher education in recording such matters. Again, I[124] humbly beg the Sisters for pardon.

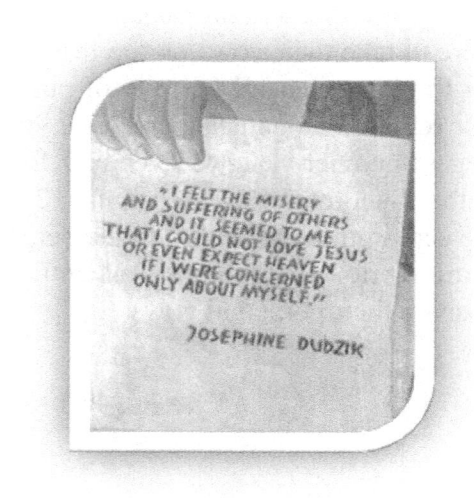

"I FELT THE MISERY AND SUFFERING OF OTHERS AND IT SEEMED TO ME THAT I COULD NOT LOVE JESUS OR EVEN EXPECT HEAVEN IF I WERE CONCERNED ONLY ABOUT MYSELF."

JOSEPHINE DUDZIK

The End

---

122   Mother herself characterizes her writing as a "Chronicle of the Community." Hence her writing is not to be considered a story of her own life. True enough there is relatively little insight into Mother's own thought in the Chronicle. We learn more of her from Sisters still living who knew her, and, of course, from her own relatives. Yet even these accounts leave much of Mother's true personality unrevealed.

123   As has been mentioned in the introduction of this typewritten manuscript, everything possible has been done in order to reproduce most faithfully the present manuscript copy of Mother, leaving all mistakes, erroneous spelling, overwritings, etc.

124   The last notes made by Mother refer to July, 1910. Mother was then 49 years old. Not much of her earthly pilgrimage remained; she died on September 20, 1918.

93

ANNOTATIONS

The preceding manuscript notes of Mother Mary Theresa are not complete if we do not give additional information.

The first General Chapter opened August 12, 1910. Most Reverend Archbishop Quigley assigned Reverend Father Director (Reverend A. Spetz) as leader of the Chapter. The first act of the Chapter was to elect the Mother General. For this office by a majority of votes, Reverend Mother Anna was elected for a term of six years. In the same way, by secret votes, the following Sisters were elected as members of the Authority: Sister M. Vincent, Assistant and first councilor, Sister M. Hedwig, second councilor, Sister Andrew, third councilor, Sister Aloysia, general secretary, Sister Salomea, general procurator.

On August 12, 1910, Mother M. Theresa resigned her office as a Superior in the Community which she held since January 1, 1909. Humanly speaking, Mother suffered from this first Chapter. She was transferred to labor in the garden, laundry and sewing room.

In addition, a new grave in St. Adalbert Cemetery was designated for Mother Mary Anna, while her previous place of rest became reserved for Mother Mary Theresa. From the sworn statements of the living members of Mother's family, who were visiting her in her last illness, one may conclude that Mother knew of the opened tomb waiting for her. She referred to it saying: "Did you at least cover the grave with boards, because it rains so hard and it may be flooded with water?"

During the last days, Mother was almost continually unconscious. From her physical appearance, it was evident she had cancerous sores which afflicted her with much suffering. Mother died September 20, 1918, at the age of 58. She spent 23 years in the convent. In a sermon delivered over her tomb, Rt. Reverend Msgr. Nawrocki said: "Whom did you come to see in this coffin?... I will tell you who, a beggar who sacrificed all she had for human misery..." May God give her a crown of eternal glory.

Father Henry Malak
Postulator of Mother Mary Theresa's Cause

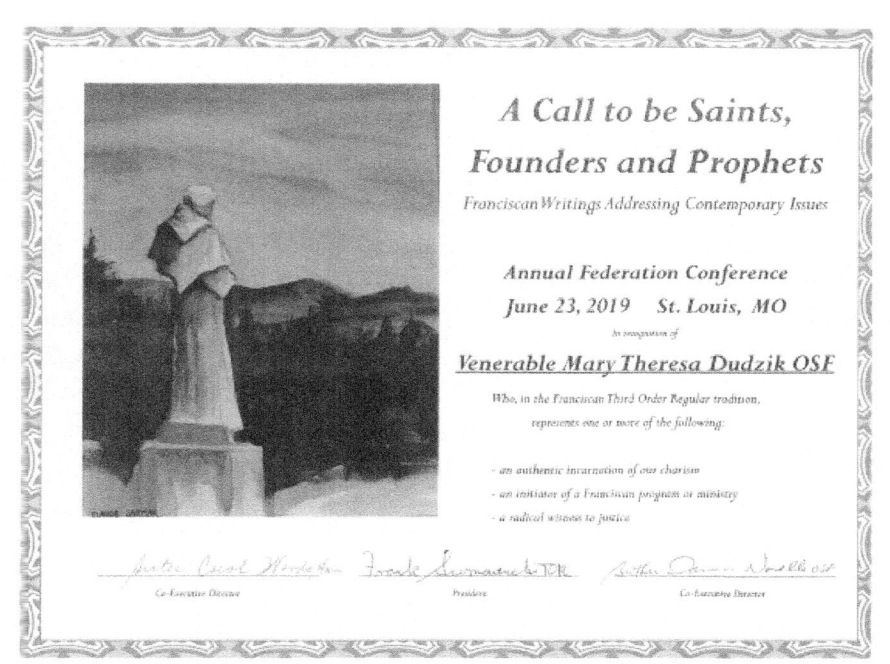

> ### A Call to be Saints, Founders and Prophets
> *Franciscan Writings Addressing Contemporary Issues*
>
> **Annual Federation Conference**
> **June 23, 2019   St. Louis, MO**
>
> *In recognition of*
>
> **Venerable Mary Theresa Dudzik OSF**
>
> *Who, in the Franciscan Third Order Regular tradition, represents one or more of the following:*
>
> - *an authentic incarnation of our charism*
> - *an initiator of a Franciscan program or ministry*
> - *a radical witness to justice*

In 2019 the Franciscan Sisters of Chicago submitted the name of their Foundress, Venerable Mary Theresa Dudzik, to be their choice of honoree for the annual Peacemaker award of the Franciscan Federation. The criteria of that year was: Honorees are TOR Franciscan brothers and sisters within a Congregation or Province who exhibit some of the following criteria:
- A Saint in our family (authentic incarnation of our TOR charism) OR
- A Founder in Franciscan tradition (initiator of a program or ministry) OR
- A Prophet in our challenging times (radical witness to justice)

In naming Mother Theresa, the Franciscan Sisters of Chicago said, "As an authentic incarnation of the spirit of St. Francis, Venerable Mary Theresa Dudzik (1860-1918), a Franciscan Tertiary, saw the poor elderly homeless on the streets of Chicago and brought them into her own apartment, giving them shelter, food, and loving care. Her heart was so touched by their plight that she surrendered her future of a comfortable life as a talented seamstress/fashion designer, to found and become a humble member of the Franciscan Sisters of Chicago in 1894 and to open the first nursing home in the city of Chicago five years later. As a prophet she spoke not only with her words, but with her whole life, that the poor, homeless, and elderly were our sisters and brothers, not garbage to be left in alleys. True to her Franciscan charism, her daughters are celebrating 125 years of ministry, having taken her original call and applied it to the issues of our times. Venerable Mary Theresa Dudzik is a Saint, Founder, and Prophet who continues to speak to our world today which yet fails to respect life for people of all cultures, ages, faiths, and economic status."

Epilogue

The Canonization Cause of Mary Theresa Dudzik, 1962-2019

Josephine Dudzik was born August 30, 1860, in Plocicz, Poland. She immigrated with her family to Chicago where they settled on the near Northside, in the parish of St. Stanislaus Kostka. Josephine became very involved in parish activities and was a member of the Third Order Secular of St. Francis of Assisi. Her kind heart noted the horrible plight of the homeless and needy elderly, and she began to shelter some of them in her apartment home which she shared with her aging mother.

As the city faced yet another cruel winter with sweeping bouts of influenza, tuberculosis, and diphtheria, Josephine turned to her companions in the Third Order, asking them for help in caring for the starving homeless. After a year of considering Josephine's request, only a handful of members agreed to help. The pastor, Rev. Vincent Barzynski, C.R., however, intervened and said he would give his blessing to the venture only if the women agreed to form a religious community, taking on the three vows, and living a community life of prayer and shared ministry. He reasoned that without the stability of a religious congregation as caretakers of these poor elderly, the current volunteers would gradually lose their initial fervor, leave the ministry, thus leaving the elderly abandoned.

Josephine agreed to the pastor's proposal and, on December 8, 1894, she took the name Sister Mary Theresa, thus founding the Franciscan Sisters of Chicago. In the ensuing years she built the first nursing home for the elderly in Chicago. On behalf of her Sisters, she also accepted the care of orphan children, and embraced the education ministry in parish elementary schools. As Sister Theresa aged into her 50s, her health deteriorated. Her personal gifts were compassion, joy, humility, and piety, and not necessarily leadership. Hence the Sisters never voted her into leadership positions, and, as the little community grew, new members never realized that the quiet older Sister working beside them, was indeed the foundress. Finally, succumbing to abdominal cancer, she died in Chicago on September 20, 1918, at the age of 58.

Rev. Henry Malak, TOR, a native of Poland and survivor of Dachau, came to the United States and enjoyed a ministry as retreat master. He preached retreats for the Franciscan Sisters of Chicago and learned of the life of the foundress. Sensing her holiness, he encouraged the Sisters to further her Cause. Normally, a guild or organization is formed to promote a cause for sainthood. The guild for our foundress was established in 1962 by Sister Venantia Rec with approval of the General Minister, Sister M. Beatrice Rybacki. Rev. Henry Malak edited the *Apostle of Mercy from Chicago*, a bulletin to acquaint the public with the life and holiness of Mother Theresa. By 1963, Rev. Malak became a researcher and advocate for her Cause, writing several books about her. He was her Postulator and worked with the Chicago Archdiocesan tribunal which examined the merits of her proposed canonization.

Sister Mary Venantia Rec served in leadership in the Congregation and devoted her later years to promoting the Cause of Mother Theresa.

From 1970-1981 an exhaustive search of Mother Theresa's writings was undertaken, a detailed biography was written, and eyewitness accounts were gathered. Mother Theresa's remains, brought to the Motherhouse of the Franciscan Sisters of Chicago in Lemont from St. Adalbert cemetery in 1972, were sealed in a granite sarcophagus in the Sacred Heart of Jesus Chapel. A special large issue of *The Apostle of Mercy from Chicago* bulletin carried the story in great detail, supplemented with numerous photographs. That issue which listed Sister Venantia and Miss Ann Dudzik as coeditors, went into three printings. Sister Jeanette Golojuch took charge of the circulation.

When sufficient information had been gathered, the investigation of the candidate, Mary Theresa Dudzik, was presented by the local bishop to the Congregation for the Causes of the Saints, who named Theresa Dudzik a Servant of God.

Six years later, in 1987, Mother Theresa's promoter, Rev. Malak, died and was buried on the Motherhouse grounds in Lemont. The Cause for her beatification and canonization, however, was actively pursued by both the Franciscan Sisters of Chicago and the Archdiocesan tribunal.

Sister Alvernia Groszek was appointed editor of the Bulletin for the League of the Servant of God Mother Mary Theresa and the first issue, dated January/February 1988, was sent out to members. Sister Kathleen Melia served as assistant editor.

Using her gift of networking with others, Sister Mary Alvernia Groszek took up the task as editor of the bulletin to spread devotion to Mother Theresa.

Witnesses were called before the tribunal to recount concrete facts regarding the exercise of Christian virtues considered heroic, that is, the theological virtues: faith, hope and charity, and the cardinal virtues: prudence, justice, temperance and fortitude, and others specific to Mother Theresa's state in life.

Once the archdiocesan investigation was finished, the acts and documentation were passed on to the Congregation for the Causes of Saints in a document called the Positio. The Positio underwent an examination (theological) by nine theologians who gave their vote. Since the majority of

Venerable Mary Thersa Dudzik, a Polish immigrant who labored in Chicago, opened the city's first nursing home

the theologians were in favor, the cause was passed on for examination by cardinals and bishops who are members of the Congregation for the Causes of Saints. Because their judgment was favorable, the prefect of the Congregation presented the results of the entire course of the Cause to the Holy Father, who gave his approval and authorized the Congregation to draft the relative decree. Thus, because of the heroic virtues evident in her life, Mother Theresa was declared Venerable on March 26, 1994, by Pope John Paul II.

Sister Venantia, who had labored so long on the Cause was blessed to have lived to see Mother Theresa progress along the steps to canonization. Sister Venantia died less than a year later, on February 27, 1995.

For the next step in achieving the beatification of a confessor (non-martyr), a miracle attributed to the Servant of God, verified after his/her death, is necessary. The required miracle must be proven through an appropriate canonical investigation. Sister Mary Francine Labus was appointed liaison to the Postulator in Rome and took on the task of collecting information about favors granted through the intercession of Mother Theresa.

Sister Mary Francine Labus used her talents of organization and communications to further the Cause.

On March 6, 2002, Mr. Andrea Ambrosi, Postulator for the Cause of Beatification of Venerable Mother Theresa Dudzik, came from Rome to interview several witnesses regarding the case of Jerry Lisiecki, a young man who was injured severely in the Illinois Central train crash in October 1972. Jerry had been in a coma and was not expected to recover. Physicians had declared he would remain in a vegetative state for the rest of his life.

Jerry's mother visited Our Lady of Victory Motherhouse during the holidays because of a "dream" she had. She took poinsettia leaves from a plant atop the sarcophagus of Mother Mary Theresa Dudzik and placed them on Jerry's five senses while she continued the Novena to Mother Theresa. At the conclusion of the nine-day novena, while she was visiting Jerry, he responded by opening his eyes and recognizing her.

This marvel, however, did not meet the requirements of the Vatican process, and in 2010 the process for the beatification of Mother Theresa stagnated.

To reach more people who might develop a strong devotion to their foundress, the Franciscan Sisters of Chicago appointed Sister Jeanne Marie Toriskie as the next liaison for the Cause. She composed multimedia presentations and began to travel to various parishes and organizations who desired to learn more about this new American saint-to-be. Sister Jeanne Marie maintained her relationship with St. Stanislaus Kostka where she had given several presentations to enthusiastic audiences. After several meetings with the pastor, Rev. Anthony Bus, C.R., he invited her to use his radio station to broadcast the holy foundress's story throughout the tri-state area that is Chicagoland. In the fall of 2012 Sister told the story of the humble woman whose compassionate heart led to the founding of a Congregation of Religious and a ministry for the poor and needy which spans the Midwest and serves thousands of people to this day.

Sister Jeanne Marie Toriskie sits at the microphone, ready to send out the story of Venerable Mary Theresa Dudzik across Chicagoland via radio.

As St. Stanislaus Kostka Parish, Mother Theresa's first home parish in the United States, planned their 150th anniversary in 2017, they determined

The new statue of Venerable Mary Theresa Dudzik stands in a prominent place in St. Stanislaus Kostka Church in Chicago where she began her works of mercy and charity.

to feature their famous parishioner. Pastor Rev. Anthony Bus, C.R., engaged artist Stefan Niedorezo to carve an original statue of Mother Theresa which would become a permanent shrine in the church. At the conclusion of the anniversary Mass, Cardinal Blase Cupich blessed the statue of Venerable Theresa.

In anticipation of the 100th death anniversary of Mother Theresa which would occur on September 20, 2018, Sister Jeanne Marie designed a series of monthly guides to help prepare for this day. Each guide included an historic image from the life of Mother Theresa, an excerpt from her Chronicle detailing a spiritual challenge that she encountered, a quotation in which she gives her response to the challenge, together with reflective questions and suggested activities which would bring her spiritual treasures to life 100 years later.

This bronze medallion, designed by artist Stefan Niedorozo to capture the image of his statue of Venerable Mary Theresa Dudzik, was issued for the 150th anniversary of St. Stanislaus Kostka Parish in Chicago, Dudzik's home parish.

The Franciscan Sisters of Chicago invited all to use these guides found on their website, http://www.chicagofranciscans.org. The pastors at St. Stanislaus Kostka Parish (Rev. Anthony Bus, C.R. at the home parish of Mother Theresa) and St. Rene Parish (Rev. Thomas Bernas[1] at his parish, due to his role as a member of the Archdiocesan Tribunal for her Cause) made these guides available to their parishioners as inserts to their Sunday bulletins from September 2017 through September 2018. Sister Diane Marie Collins who was working in campus ministry used these guides with the students at the University of Illinois Chicago campus. The guides were also used at all the facilities of Franciscan Ministries, the corporate-sponsored ministries of the Franciscan Sisters of Chicago.

---

1 Fr. Bernas is currently at St. Stephen Deacon and Martyr Parish in Tinley Park, IL.

Today there is technology available to share the story of Mother Theresa Dudzik with the entire global community. The Franciscan Sisters of Chicago have established their own website which publicizes their foundress. In addition, they have a website solely devoted to her Cause at mothertheresadudzik.com. Mother Theresa also has her own Facebook page.

For those who would wish to further their knowledge and devotion to Mother Theresa, her website makes a number of materials available:

- A short biography of her life entitled, "*A Heart for Jesus*"
- A novena prayer and beatification prayer leaflet
- A brochure summarizing the major events in the progress of her Cause
- A prayer card containing an original prayer composed by Mother Theresa.
- A medallion containing soil from the grave of Venerable Theresa from her original internment at St. Adalbert cemetery in Niles, IL
- A spiritual enrollment card which assures the petitioner of Masses and the prayers of the Sisters for their loved one for an entire year. The card features Mother Theresa's image.

Among the beautiful treasures of the past, however, is the original chronology of Mother Theresa, written in her own hand in her native Polish language. The Chronicle was translated into English under the direction of Rev. Malak and the Sisters. In 2015 the English version was transferred into a digital format and was published for dissemination via the Internet. Its release was the 125th anniversary of the Franciscan Sisters of Chicago, December 8, 2019.

[Handwritten Polish prayer text, partially damaged:]

... Pod Twoją obronę uciekamy się itd.

V. Dałeś nam Panie chleb z nieba
R. Wszelką słodycz mający w sobie
V. Ześlij nam Panie Ducha Twego św.
R. A odnowisz postać ziemi
V. Módl się za nami św. Boża Rodzicielko
R. Abyśmy się stali godnymi obietnic P. Chr.

   Módlmy się

Boże, któryś nam w cudownym Sakramencie, pamiątkę Męki swej zostawić raczył, daj nam, abyśmy tak Ciała i Krwi Twojej święte Tajemnice czcili, żebyśmy skutków odkupienia naszego w nas zawsze doznawali. Boże, któryś serca wiernych swoich światłem Ducha świętego oświecił, daj nam w tymże Duchu co prawe jest znosić, poznawać, a pociechą, która najwyższa, nieustannie się weselić. Łaskę Twoją prosimy Panie, racz wlać w serca nasze abyśmy, którzy za zwiastowaniem anielskim Chrystusa Syna Twego wcielenie poznali, przez Mękę Jego i Krzyż do chwały zmartwychwstania byli doprowadzeni. Przez zasługi Ojca św. Franciszka...

Sr. M. Teresa

The original *Prayer for Our Daily Needs* written and signed by Venerable Theresa Dudzik in Polish, her native language. She wrote this prayer on the fly-leaf of her prayer book. The English translation is on the next page.

Appendix A

A Prayer for Our Daily Needs

O GOD,
you have enriched your Church
with a religious family,
the Franciscan Sisters of Chicago.
Give us the grace
to reject the goods of this world
and to direct our desires to heavenly things.
We ask your mercy;
forgive us our sins.
Through the intercession of
the Blessed Virgin Mary
and all your saints,
especially St. Francis of Assisi,
keep us your faithful servants,
our families, relatives, friends and benefactors
in constant holiness.
Cleanse us from our sins
and adorn us with virtue.
Grant us peace and salvation.
Deliver us from our enemies,
seen and unseen.
Help us to overcome our bodily desires.
Provide us with healthful air and fertile land.
Support our friends with love;
look kindly upon our enemies.
Keep our country,
Chicago our city,
and all the faithful who live here
from flood, famine, fire, war,
and especially from loss of faith in you.

-Mother Mary Theresa Dudzik, OSF

Appendix B

Beatification Prayer
for the Venerable
Mother Mary Theresa Dudzik

Heavenly Father,
you inflamed the compassionate heart
of Mother Mary Theresa
with the heroic virtues
of charity and mercy.

If it is your will,
may she be declared Blessed
for your honor and glory
and may she inspire others
to imitate her love
for the needy, poor
and suffering of our world.

This we ask through Christ our Lord.
Amen.

Published with ecclesiastical approval
Francis Cardinal George
1 May 2002

Appendix C

Novena Prayer through the intercession of the Venerable Mother Mary Theresa Dudzik

Venerable Servant of God,
Mother Mary Theresa,
during your lifetime you practiced
great charity and later wrote:
"I felt the misery and suffering of others
and was constantly occupied
with the thought of
how I could be of service
to the needy and the poor."

I, who venerate you,
come to you for help.
Venerable Servant of God,
Mother Mary Theresa,
beg for me at the throne of God,
for this, my special intention
(mention petition)
through Christ our Lord.
Amen.

Appendix D

How St. Francis Asked For and Obtained the Indulgence of Forgiveness

He awoke one night in 1216 at the Portiuncula and an inspiration stronger than usual prompted him to arise and go into the little chapel. He knelt in prayer and, as he prayed, our Lord, accompanied by His Mother, appeared to him and bade him ask for that which he desired most. "O God," he said, "although I am a great sinner, I beseech You to grant a full pardon of all sins to all who, having repented and confessed their sins, shall visit this church." And Jesus said to him: "Francis, you ask much, but you are worthy of greater things, and greater things you shall have."

Our Lord then granted Francis' request and told him to go to His Vicar for ratification of the indulgence. Honorius III, who was just beginning his Pontificate, was holding court at Perugia, and it was to him that Francis presented his petition.

Honorius was a spiritual, unworldly man, yet at such a request he hesitated. "Holy Father," Francis said urgently, "a little while ago I restored a chapel for you in honor of the Virgin Mother of Christ (the Portiuncula), and I beseech you to bestow on it an indulgence."

"For how many years do you want this indulgence?" the Pontiff inquired. "Holy Father," said Francis, "I ask not for years but for souls." "Just what do you want?" Honorius asked. "Holy Father," replied Francis, "the Lord has commanded me to ask you that all those who after confession shall visit the Portiuncula with contrite hearts may obtain full remission of the punishment due to the sins of their whole lives from the day of Baptism to the day they enter this church." Honorius pondered the extraordinary request and said slowly three times: "I also, in the name of God, grant you the indulgence."

Honorius wanted to give Francis the document of the indulgence, but Francis saw no need for it. "What have you to show that this indulgence has been granted you?" the Pope asked in amazement as Francis prepared to depart for Assisi without any written confirmation of the great permission. "Holy Father," he replied, "Your word is enough for me. If this is the work of God, it is for Him to make His work manifest. I desire no other document. The Blessed Virgin Mary shall be the charter, Christ the notary, and the angels the witnesses." Some days later, before the Bishops of Umbria, Francis said: "Brethren, I want to send you all to Heaven!"

http://www.franciscanfriarstor.com/archive/stfrancis/stf_portuncula_ indulgence.htm

Appendix E

Chronological List of Quotations from Venerable Mother Mary Theresa Dudzik

QUOTATION	PAGE
I felt the misery and sufferings of others; and it seemed to me that I could not love Jesus, or even expect heaven, if I were concerned only about myself and my mother—not to suffer any inconvenience, but simply to live in comfort.	3
Very often I felt a persistent urge to make greater sacrifices for others.	4
I was especially guided with a continuous thought of how I could be of service to the needy and the poor.	4
Father said that we were not allowed to oppose a good cause, but we should promote it and help in bringing it to a successful fruition.	6
It then occurred to me that St. Francis had no permanent quarters either; and this thought brought me peace of mind.	7
Since the novena was to be offered in our intention, we began it with the greatest devotion and begged the Mother of God for help in this difficult undertaking which now confronted us.	7
He also demanded a promise from me that I would care for this Community not only in its time of prosperity but also in times of trouble; and when difficulties would beset it from all sides.	8
The thought that I deliberately agreed on this undertaking for Jesus Christ is still an incentive till this day for me.	8
It was my first act of self-denial for this cause, and it cost me very much.	12
Everyone had work suitable to her abilities.	12
Yet, when it was necessary to sacrifice myself in order to bring peace, I did not hesitate; I went forth, trusting in the good God, and He came to my aid.	13

QUOTATION	PAGE
I strove to choose the hardest task. I note this, not to praise myself, but to reveal God's evident assistance.	14
I was of a happy disposition, and I never liked crying of any kind.	15
I offered it all to Jesus, hoping that better times would soon come.	15
We began again with renewed zeal and fervor. However, we needed more than that; we needed extra hands to help us.... But God helped us here, too.	17
And the Lord was helping me.	18
We continued working to attain the goal for which we had banded together.	18
In spite of everything, I did not lose my happy disposition and detected the Will of God in everything.	19
Since I had given my consent freely, my burdens became light and I never lost courage. I tried to continue working for this community most energetically.	19
We could only place our trust in God; to hope solely in Him was the safest course.	20
When I was notified that my services were no longer needed, I cried in secret, unnoticed by anyone except the Lord Jesus.	21
However, life has a way of going on amidst the sorrows and joys that befall us.	22
I had never thought that it would ever be necessary for me to beg money for my own upkeep and also for the project to which I had dedicated my life.	23
After he gave me his blessing, he instructed me to accept all the money as a donation for the Home for the Aged and Invalids; and to accept all rudeness for myself. I was greatly inspired by these words.	23

QUOTATION	PAGE
Despite all the difficulties and troubles, I never felt completely exhausted. My greatest joy was when I knelt down to say the evening prayers and rosary with the residents and saw how fervently and willingly they participated in the religious exercises, although the situation was quite the reverse when they first came to us.	28
It seemed to me that God was pleased, even with the little good that I could do for His glory.	28
God was ever ready to help us. St. Joseph, too, who was chosen as the patron of our group and our project from its very inception, aided us in all our needs both temporal and spiritual. We never sought the help of God or St. Joseph in vain, even though we did have to seek aid quite often.	29
I firmly believe that St. Joseph would grant succor to anyone in need.	29
It was necessary that I submit everything to the Will of God.	30
I only wished that God's Will be done; I placed all my trust in Him and would readily submit to His designs.	34
Life here was quite similar to the one led by the Holy Family in the cave in Bethlehem.	36
It always happens that God sends sorrow, but He also sends consolation.	37
Nevertheless, I didn't feel too bad, knowing that such is the Will of God; and that He would continue to enrich me with His graces if I only would continue to cooperate with Him and benefit spiritually from His goodness.	37
And so the Lord helped us to move successfully.	38
St. Joseph remembered us in so many instances.	42
I still felt like a fish removed from water without the presence of the Blessed Sacrament.	43
At times I felt such a great yearning for Jesus in the Blessed Sacrament that I was ready to run to church, even late in the evening.	44
The longing for Jesus would persist and return often.	44

QUOTATION	PAGE
Truthfully, we were delighted at the thought of beginning our postulancy; and I was so overwhelmed by it that I wished to honor my favorite feast of the Mother of God more solemnly.	45
It (my thought) was about obtaining an organ so that we could, here in this deserted place and in our home, play and sing together at Midnight Mass in honor of the Child Jesus; so that we could thank Him for all the graces.	46
I tried to bear these jeers patiently at home, although at times misunderstandings and quarrels were the consequence.	48
And I would reassure myself, as much as I was able, thinking that whatever I did I wanted to do it for the greater glory of God.	49
But I promised God and him, after some deliberation, so long as I would live I would try, as much as my strength would endure, not to give such scandal.	49
The only thing that I could do, I thought to myself, was to pray that God would change all of this. Therefore, I began to present our difficulties to Jesus more often in order to expect help from Him only.	49
God did not forsake or forget us.	51
We were to have the Blessed Sacrament in our chapel. That was a privilege for which we were very delighted.	51
We did not waver but had hope in God.	53
It was necessary to forget the sorrow and to occupy ourselves with a greater energy with our husbandry and charges.	54
I couldn't contain my joy at the thought that from this day we would have the Blessed Sacrament in our small chapel.	55
Now we would be able to associate more frequently with the Lord Jesus, so close in our midst, and present our various anxieties to Him.	55
My doubt disappeared after I placed myself entirely in submission to the Will of God.	62

QUOTATION	PAGE
Those criticisms of my conduct were no small advantage for my pride. I would want to bear more as long as God would not be offended, and I would consider it even great happiness to be able to suffer for the greater glory of God and the good of this Community.	64
We received the Office for the first time on September 8, 1901. It seemed to us as if a new life was begun.	67

Appendix F

List of Illustrations

SOURCE	DESCRIPTION	PAGE
Archives of the Franciscan Sisters of Chicago (FSC).	Black and white photograph of Venerable Mary Theresa Dudzik.	Front cover and title page
FSC commissioned graphic work by Steve Kozy of Franciscan Ministries, Lemont IL.	Overall cover design is based on a stained glass window in the Sacred Heart Chapel of Our Lady of Victory Motherhouse in Lemont IL. The window was designed by artist Claire M. Wing of Dallas, TX.	Front cover and title page
Adapted from Istkart [CC BY-SA 4.0 (https://creativecommons.org/licenses/by-sa/4.0)], from Wikimedia Commons https://commons.wikimedia.org/wiki/File:Europe._Historical_map_AD_1864.svg	Map of the partitioning of Poland in 1864.	vii
FSC commissioned India ink drawing by Walter Krawiec originally published in *Theresa of Chicago* by Reverend Henry M. Malak, Uncle Gutenburg Press, Toronto, Canada, 1975.	Parish church of Sts. Peter and Paul in Kamien Krajenski, Poland.	vii
Google Maps.	Map of Poland.	viii

SOURCE	DESCRIPTION	PAGE
Archives of the Franciscan Sisters of Chicago.	Black and white photograph of the Dudzik family circa 1890.	viii
Archives of the Franciscan Sisters of Chicago.	Close-up of Agnes Dudzik, mother of Venerable Mary Theresa Dudzik, from the original black and white photograph of the Dudzik family circa 1890.	ix
FSC commissioned oil painting by artist Walter Krawiec.	Oil painting of Venerable Mary Theresa Dudzik holding the Constitutions of her new Religious congregation, with the Blessed Virgin Mary in the background.	x
https://commons.wikimedia.org/wiki/File:Haymarket_explosion.jpg USA public domain image.	Image of the Haymarket riot.	xi
https://commons.wikimedia.org/wiki/File:Bellows_CliffDwellers.jpg	"Cliff Dwellers," May 1913, oil on canvas by George Bellows.	xii
https://commons.wikimedia.org/wiki/File:Elements_of_transportation,_a_discussion_of_steam_railroad_electric_railway,_and_ocean_and_inland_water_transportation_(1920)_(14757591691).jpg	Map of the United States Showing Railroads in 1890.	xii
https://en.wikipedia.org/wiki/World%27s_Columbian_Exposition#/media/File:1893_world_columbian_exposition.jpg	Advertisement piece of art for the World's Columbian Exposition (also known as the Chicago World's Fair), held in 1893.	xiii

SOURCE	DESCRIPTION	PAGE
https://commons.wikimedia.org/wiki/File:PULLMAN07.jpg	Picture by G.A. Coffin entitled "Deputies Trying to Move an Engine and Car on the Chicago, Rock Island, and Pacific Railroad at Blue Island, July 2, 1894".	xiv
Archives of the Franciscan Sisters of Chicago.	Image of St. Stanislaus Kostka parish, Chicago, circa 1890.	xv
https://upload.wikimedia.org/wikipedia/commons/thumb/a/ae/Helena_Modrzejewska_by_Melecjusz_Dutkiewicz.jpg/220px-Helena_Modrzejewska_by_Melecjusz_Dutkiewicz.jpg USA public domain image.	Image of actress Helen Modrzejewski.	xvi
Archives of the Franciscan Sisters of Chicago.	Black and white photograph of Josephine Dudzik circa 1890.	xvii
FSC commissioned India ink drawing by Walter Krawiec originally published in *Theresa of Chicago* by Reverend Henry M. Malak, Gutenburg Press, Toronto, Canada, 1975.	India ink rendition of Pastor Reverend Barzynski and Josephine Dudzik in the doorway of the basement of St. Stanislaus Kostka parish church in Chicago, discussing the plight of the homeless sheltered there.	xviii

SOURCE	DESCRIPTION	PAGE
FSC commissioned India ink drawing by Walter Krawiec.	Oil painting of Venerable Mary Theresa Dudzik holding the Constitutions of her new Religious congregation, with St. Stanislaus Kostka parish in the background with the Sacred Heart.	xxi
Archives of the Franciscan Sisters of Chicago.	Photograph of Reverend Henry Maria Malak, postulator of the Cause of Mary Theresa Dudzik.	xxii
FSC commissioned India ink drawing by Walter Krawiec originally published in *Theresa of Chicago* by Reverend Henry M. Malak, Gutenburg Press, Toronto, Canada, 1975.	India ink rendition of the apartment building in Chicago where Josephine Dudzik resided with her parents.	3
FSC commissioned white Cararra marble statue by an unknown artist.	Color photograph of the top of the marble statue of Josephine Dudzik on the campus of Our Lady of Victory Motherhouse in Lemont, IL.	5
https://upload.wikimedia. org/wikipedia/commons/ thumb/5/55/Archbishop_ Feehan.jpg/220px- Archbishop_Feehan.jpg USA public domain image.	Image of Archbishop Patrick Augustine Feehan.	9
https://commons. wikimedia.org/wiki/ File Oplatki.w.koszyczku.jpg	Christmas wafer on a basket.	10

SOURCE	DESCRIPTION	PAGE
FSC commissioned graphic work by Steve Kozy of Franciscan Ministries, Lemont IL.	Combined images of trunk, lock, and key.	11
FSC commissioned India ink drawing by Walter Krawiec originally published in *Theresa of Chicago* by Reverend Henry M. Malak, Uncle Gutenburg Press, Toronto, Canada, 1975.	India ink rendition of Josephine Dudzik, seamstress and tailor.	14
Sister Jeanne Marie Toriskie, OSF, Ph.D.	Photograph of decorated Easter eggs owned by Sister M. Bernadette Bajuscik, OSF.	15
Sister Jeanne Marie Toriskie, OSF, Ph.D.	Photograph of Josephine Dudzik from the carved wood bas relief triptych created by artist Stefan Niedorezo, housed at St. Stanislaus Kostka rectory.	20
FSC commissioned India ink drawing by Walter Krawiec originally published in *Theresa of Chicago* by Reverend Henry M. Malak, Uncle Gutenburg Press, Toronto, Canada, 1975.	India ink rendition of Josephine Dudzik in Chicago.	24
Sister Jeanne Marie Toriskie, OSF, Ph.D.	Photograph of Reverend Vincent Barzynski, C.R., from the carved wood bas relief triptych created by artist Stefan Niedorezo, housed at St. Stanislaus Kostka rectory.	24

SOURCE	DESCRIPTION	PAGE
FSC commissioned India ink drawing by Walter Krawiec originally published in *Theresa of Chicago* by Reverend Henry M. Malak, Uncle Gutenburg Press, Toronto, Canada, 1975.	India ink rendition of the Chicago homeless who turned to Josephine Dudzik for help.	25
Sister Jeanne Marie Toriskie, OSF, Ph.D.	Photograph of early wheelchair from St. Joseph Home in Chicago, now on display in the Heritage Hall in Lemont IL.	26
FSC commissioned white Cararra marble statue by an unknown artist.	Photograph of the marble statue of Josephine Dudzik on the campus of Our Lady of Victory Motherhouse in Lemont, IL.	27
Gift of Gary Duckett to FSC.	Image of an 1897 U.S. penny.	29
FSC commissioned India ink drawing by Walter Krawiec originally published in *Theresa of Chicago* by Reverend Henry M. Malak, Uncle Gutenburg Press, Toronto, Canada, 1975.	India ink rendition of Sister Theresa Dudzik atop the new St. Joseph Home under construction.	35
Public domain image. https://www.wpclipart.com/animals/birds/C/chicken/Rhode_Island_Red.jpg.html	Image of backyard chicken.	36
https://www.flickr.com/photos/	Image of a stove newly available for purchase in 1898.	38

SOURCE	DESCRIPTION	PAGE
FSC commissioned India ink drawing by Walter Krawiec originally published in *Theresa of Chicago* by Reverend Henry M. Malak, Uncle Gutenburg Press, Toronto, Canada, 1975.	India ink rendition of Sister Theresa Dudzik driving the horse and wagon filled with groceries for the homeless at St. Joseph Home in unincorporated Avondale.	40
FSC commissioned India ink drawing by Walter Krawiec originally published in *Theresa of Chicago* by Reverend Henry M. Malak, Uncle Gutenburg Press, Toronto, Canada, 1975.	India ink rendition of Sister Theresa Dudzik with the newly-purchased cow to provide fresh milk for the homeless at St. Joseph Home in unincorporated Avondale.	41
https://www.wpclipart.com/food/vegetables/carrot/carrot_bunch.png.html Public domain image.	Image of carrots.	43
FSC commissioned India ink drawing by Walter Krawiec originally published in *Theresa of Chicago* by Reverend Henry M. Malak, Uncle Gutenburg Press, Toronto, Canada, 1975.	India ink rendition of Rev. Vincent Barzynski, C.R., spiritual advisor to Sister Theresa Dudzik.	52
FSC commissioned India ink drawing by Walter Krawiec originally published in *Theresa of Chicago* by Reverend Henry M. Malak, Uncle Gutenburg Press, Toronto, Canada, 1975.	India ink rendition of Rev. Andrew Spetz, C.R., who succeeded Reverend Barzynski as spiritual advisor to Sister Theresa Dudzik.	54

SOURCE	DESCRIPTION	PAGE
Archives of the Franciscan Sisters of Chicago.	Photograph of the First Profession of the first Franciscan Sisters of Blessed Kunegunda, with Sister Theresa Dudzik at the far right.	57
FSC commissioned India ink drawing by Walter Krawiec originally published in *Theresa of Chicago* by Reverend Henry M. Malak, Uncle Gutenburg Press, Toronto, Canada, 1975.	India ink rendition of Sister Theresa Dudzik holding an orphan boy.	58
https://upload.wikimedia.org/wikipedia/commons/5/50/St_Hedwig_Chicago.JPG	Image of St. Hedwig Church in Chicago, IL.	64
http://www.bcrnews.com/_internal/cimg!0/	Image of Sts. Peter and Paul Church in Spring Valley, IL.	66
Sister Jeanne Marie Toriskie, OSF, Ph.D.	Photograph of an iconic image of St. Kinga (Kunegunda) paired with a vessel of salt topped by wedding bands.	72
Archives of the Franciscan Sisters of Chicago.	Close-up of Agnes Dudzik, mother of Venerable Mary Theresa Dudzik, from the original photograph of the Dudzik family, circa 1890.	74
Archives of the Franciscan Sisters of Chicago.	Photograph of Venerable Mary Theresa Dudzik.	80
https://www.wpclipart.com/medical/symbols/Caduceus_red.png.html Public domain image.	Image of caduceus, symbol of medicine.	83

SOURCE	DESCRIPTION	PAGE
https://www.wpclipart.com/holiday/Christmas/candles/candles_2/candle_lit.png.html Public domain image.	Image of a burning candle.	84
FSC commissioned India ink drawing by Walter Krawiec originally published in *Theresa of Chicago* by Reverend Henry M. Malak, Uncle Gutenburg Press, Toronto, Canada, 1975.	India ink rendition of Sister Theresa Dudzik praying outdoors.	85
FSC commissioned India ink drawing by Walter Krawiec originally published in *Theresa of Chicago* by Reverend Henry M. Malak, Uncle Gutenburg Press, Toronto, Canada, 1975.	India ink rendition of Sister Theresa Dudzik planning the spiritual renewal of the Community in preparation for its first General Chapter.	87
https://www.wpclipart.com/music/notation/treble_staff_with_notes_01.png.html Public domain image.	Image of musical notes.	88
Sister Jeanne Marie Toriskie, OSF, Ph.D.	Photograph of Josephine Dudzik holding a scroll with her inspiration statement from the carved wood triptych created by artist Stefan Niedorezo, housed at St. Stanislaus Kostka rectory.	92

SOURCE	DESCRIPTION	PAGE
Work by artist J. Spoelstra, originally displayed at St. Anthony Medical Center in Crown Point, IN, and currently housed at the entrance of Heritage Hall in Our Lady of Victory Convent, Lemont, IL.	Oil painting of Mother Theresa Dudzik and those who sought her help.	93
Archives of the Franciscan Sisters of Chicago.	Annual Peacemaker Award certificate awarded by the Franciscan Federation on June 23, 2019.	95
Amazon.com	Book cover.	97
Archives of the Franciscan Sisters of Chicago, taken by an unknown photographer.	Photograph of Sr. M. Venantia Rec.	97
Archives of the Franciscan Sisters of Chicago, taken by an unknown photographer.	Photograph of Sr. M. Alvernia Groszek.	98
Archives of the Franciscan Sisters of Chicago, taken by an unknown photographer.	Photograph of Venerable M. Theresa Dudzik.	98
Archives of the Franciscan Sisters of Chicago, taken by an unknown photographer.	Photograph of Sr. M. Francine Labus.	99
Personal collection of Sr. Jeanne Marie Toriskie, taken by an unknown photographer.	Photograph of Sr. Jeanne Marie Toriskie at the radio station in St. Stanislaus Kostka rectory.	100
Photographed by Sr. Jeanne Marie Toriskie; original statue in St. Stanislaus Kostka Church in Chicago IL.	Photograph of statue of Mother Theresa Dudzik made by artist Stefan Niedorezo.	100

SOURCE	DESCRIPTION	PAGE
Photographed by Sr. Jeanne Marie Toriskie; original medallion in the archives of the Franciscan Sisters of Chicago.	Photograph of medallion of Mother Theresa Dudzik made by artist Stefan Niedorezo.	101
Photographed by Tim McLaughlin, Communications Coordinator for the Franciscan Sisters of Chicago; original book in Heritage Hall, Lemont IL.	Flyleaf of the Little Office of the Blessed Virgin Mary on which Mother Theresa Dudzik wrote her original "Prayer for Our Daily Needs."	103
Photographed by Tim McLaughlin, Communications Coordinator for the Franciscan Sisters of Chicago; original on display in the Franciscan Ministries Administration Building, Lemont IL.	Bas-relief of St. Francis by artist Alison Aragon, commissioned by the Franciscan Sisters of Chicago, owned by Franciscan Ministries, Lemont IL.	108
Color photograph by Sister Jeanne Marie Toriskie, OSF, Ph.D.	Image of congregational pin with logo designed by Sister M. Sponsa Bajorek, OSF	113
One of a series of six stained glass windows featuring the Blessed Virgin Mary, created by an unknown artist, commissioned by FSC, and restored by Daprato Rigali Studios of Chicago. Color photograph by Sister Mary Helene Galuszka, OSF.	Stained glass window depicting Mother Theresa and the first two Sisters seeking the help of Our Lady of Victory in the spiritual and corporal works of the Congregation. The window from the earlier 1963 Motherhouse now illumines the second floor of the current Motherhouse in Lemont.	125

SOURCE	DESCRIPTION	PAGE
FSC commissioned work by Steve Kozy of Franciscan Ministries, Lemont IL.	Photograph of an autumn view of the exterior of the current Motherhouse. Overall cover design is based on stained glass window in the Sacred Heart Chapel of Our Lady of Victory Motherhouse in Lemont IL. The window was designed by artist Claire M. Wing of Dallas, TX.	Back cover

Index

A

Aged; care of the aged and crippled ix, 6, 19, 21, 25, 26, 30, 37, 42, 54, 57, 61, 67, 69, 71, 76, 80, 96
Agnes, Sr. Mary (Josephine Roszak) 56, 62, 66, 70, 76
Aloysia, Sr. Mary (Estelle Holysz) 59, 68, 75, 77, 79, 85, 94
Ambrosi, Mr. Andrea 99
Andrew, Sr. Mary (Monica Zawadzka) 59, 94
Angelina, Sr. Mary (Constance Topolinski) 7, 9, 10, 12, 17, 18, 56, 61, 73, 76, 78, 85
Anna, Sister/Mother Mary (Rose Wisinski) 4, 5, 9, 10, 19, 20, 22, 24, 25, 26, 31, 32, 33, 34, 35, 36, 37, 41, 43, 51, 56, 61, 71, 78, 94
Antonina, Sr. Mary (Catherine Osinski) 78, 81
Approval 25, 31, 55
Arch-confraternity of the Immaculate Heart of Mary 33
Augustine, Sr. Mary (Anna Malinowski) 74
Avondale xviii, 6, 19, 27, 31, 35, 38, 69

B

Bajuscik, Sr. Bernadette, 118
Barbara, Sr. Mary (Mary Grochola) 77, 80, 85
Barzynski, Rev. Joseph 15
Barzynski, Rev. Vincent, C.R. xviii, xix, 3, 6, 12, 14, 18, 20, 22, 24, 26, 30, 34, 40, 42, 44, 48, 50, 51, 53, 67, 96
Bellows, George 115
Benigna, Sr. Mary (Frances Jakaitis) 78, 83
Berlin, WI 73, 76, 81
Bernadine, Sr. Mary (Mary Narozna) 89
Bernas, Rev. Thomas 101

Bielinski, Mr. 22
Blessed Sacrament 40, 43, 51, 55, 56, 60
Bonaventure, Sr. Mary (Francis Blazek) 70, 78, 80
Boniface, Sr. Mary (Magdalen Pranko) 85
Breszman, Mr. 56
Brigid, Sr. Mary (Victoria Czuj) 80, 88
Bubacz, Mr. 63
Building Committee 22, 24, 28, 30, 38, 41
Bus, C.R., Rev. Anthony 100, 101

C

Cajetan, Sr. Mary (Sophie Tabasz) 76
Casimir, Sr. Mary (Mary Janowiak) 88
Catechism 73
Cause for Canonization 96
Chester, Sr.Mary (Martha Dziarnowski) 79, 84
Chicago, IL 73
Children 73
Clara, Sr. Mary (Maryann Ogurek) 37, 43, 45, 46, 56, 59, 62, 65, 66, 70, 73, 76
Cleveland, OH 70, 76
Coffin, G.A. 116
Colette, Sr. Mary (Frances Nowak) 77, 80, 84
Collins, Sr. Diane Marie 101
Constitution 44, 55, 86
Cragin, IL 6, 68, 75, 76, 78

D

Dabrowski, Rev. Stephen 63
Daprato Rigali Studios of Chicago 124
Delphine, Sr. Mary (Anna Miszewski) 84
Dembinski, Rev. 65
Dominic, Sr. Mary (Rosalie Makowski) 77
Duckett, Gary 119
Dudzik Family vii, xv, 94
   Agnes Dudzik 74
   Anna Dudzik viii, 96, 97
   Frances Dudzik viii, ix
   John Dudzik ix

Joseph Dudzik 39
Josephine Dudzik (Mother Mary Theresa) vii, xiii, xv, xvi, xxi, 5, 10, 78, 80, 82, 85, 89, 94
Rosalie Dudzik 32
Rose Dudzik vii, viii

E

Elizabeth, Sr. Mary (Caroline Baut) 37, 56

F

Feehan, Archbishop Patrick Augustine 9, 55
Felixa, Sr. Mary (Stella Karwata) 62, 67, 73, 76
Filipski, Rev. 82

G

Gagala, Josephine 25
Galuszka, Sr. Helene 124
Gary, IN 88
General Chapter 86, 87, 90, 94
Gerarda, Sr.Mary (Mary Gorzkowski) 77
Gieburowski, Rev. J. 58, 64
Gnielinski, Rev. 77
Gniot, Mr. P. John 22, 24, 31, 38, 41
Golojuch, Sr. Mary Jeanette 97
Goralski, Br. Adalbert 45, 46, 60
Greenhouse 79
Groszek, Sr. Alvernia 98

H

Habits 7, 17, 55, 56, 57, 63
Hanley Mrs. H. 90
Hedwig, Sr. Mary (Rosalie Kubera) 59, 80, 85, 94
Hegewisch 84, 88
Holy Rosary Confraternity/Sodality xv, 4, 32, 33, 36, 45, 56
Hyacinth, Sr. Mary (Miss Barczewski) 73, 76

I

Ignatia, Sr. Mary (Anastasia Dukowski) 76
Independent Church 15, 16
Indiana Harbor 81, 88
Infirmary 71, 81

J

Jedrzejek, Mr. W. 22, 32
Jerome, Sr. Mary (Anna Dadej) 88
Joey, legless orphan 27
Jolanta, Sr. Mary (Joanna Nowak) 77, 79, 81
Josepha, Sr. Mary (Philomena Suchomski) 61

K

Kaczmarek, Mr. 56
Karnowski, Mrs. Elizabeth 25
Kasprzycki, Rev. O.J. 60, 63
Kielczynski, Mr. 25
Kiolbassa, Mr. Peter 20, 22, 31
Kobrzynski, Rev. Simon 11, 21, 22
Kochanski, Mr. 60
Konkowski, Frances 25
Kowalczyk, Rev. 65
Kozlowski, Rev. 17
Kozy, Steve 114, 118, 125
Krawiec, Walter 114, 115, 117, 119, 120, 122
Krolikowski, Mr. Aloysius 58
Kunegunda, Blessed 72, 82, 90
Kunegunda, Sr. (Marianna Pinkowska) 59, 63, 66, 81
Kuszynski, Rev. 59
Kwasigroch, Mr. and daughter 46

L

Labus, Sr. Mary Francine 99
Ladislaus, Sr. Mary (Mary Wroblewski) 83
Ladom, Rev. 84
Lafayette, IN 78, 82

Lagodzinska, Mr. 42, 54
Leocodia, Sr. Mary (Antoinette Das) 81
Leona, Sr. Mary (Bernice Pochelski) 76
Lewandowski, Mr. John 26, 27
Lisiecki, Jerry 99

M

Maca, Mr. John 22
Malak, Rev. Henry Malak xxii, 94, 97, 102
Mary, Sr. (Anna Welter) 43, 56, 59, 66, 75, 76, 79, 88
Matuszewski, Rev. Florian 55
McLaughlin, Timothy 124
Melia, Sr. Kathleen 98
Michael, Sr. Mary (Apolonia Sobieszczyk) 74
Midnight Mass 60
Modrzejewski, Helen xvi
Moldoon, Archbishop 83
Music 88

N

Nawrocki, Msgr. 94
Needy and the poor 4
Niedorezo, Stefan 101, 118, 122-124
Novitiate 51, 55, 56, 62, 63, 65, 68, 70, 72, 75, 78, 80, 81, 87, 90
Nursing 83

O

Orphanage 58, 59, 67, 72, 76, 83, 86, 96
Oshkosh, WI 77, 88
Osinski, Angela 41
Our Lady of Victory 56

P

Palubicki, Mr. 19
Patricia, Sr. Mary (Lauretta Eiress) 77
Paul, Sr. Mary (Mary Kirschbaum) 89
Pharmacist 78, 83
Philipina, Sr. Mary (Cecilia Lama) 62, 68, 75, 76

Philomena, Sr. Mary (Anna Marszalkowski) 76
Piechowski, Rev. John 25, 31, 57
Piotrowski, Mr. 33
Polenz, Mr. 22
Portiuncula 71, 107
Postulancy 45, 47, 56, 68, 71, 74, 78, 80, 89
Prayer vi, 104, 105, 106

Q

Quigley, Archbishop xv, 72, 86, 94

R

Radziejewski, Rev. John 22
Rapacz, Father O. 43
Rapacz, Rev. W. 65
Rec, Sr. Mary Venantia 97, 99
Rhode, Bishop P. P. 89
Rodowicz, Rev. Victor 83
Rogalski, Rev. S., C.R. 67, 87
Rose, Sr. Mary (Maryann Gorska) 59, 73, 78
Rybacki, Sr. Mary Beatrice 97

S

Saborosz, Rev. 91
Salesia, Sr. Mary (Kathryn Rzeszutko) 88
Salomea, Sr. Mary (Martha Grabowski) 61, 70, 73, 76, 81, 94
School 66, 68, 70, 73, 77, 80, 81, 84, 88, 90, 96
Sedlaczek, Rev. 40, 42
Seraphine, Sr. Mary (Martha Zamrowski) 70, 76, 88
Siara, Rev. 89
Siatka, Rev. 65
Silence 45, 47, 64
Simon, Archbishop 75
Spetz, Rev. Andrew, C.R. 44, 46, 50, 54, 57, 63, 65, 67, 71, 80, 82, 85, 87, 89, 94
Spetz, Rev. Theobald, C.R. 86
Spoelstra, J. 123

Spring Valley 66, 69, 70, 90
Stanislaus, Sr. Mary (Barbara Reich) 61, 63, 76, 87
Stanislawowski, Mr. 52
St. Ann Hospital/Infirmary 71
St. Casimir School 77
St. Elizabeth Nursery 73, 76
St. Hedwig Parish 15, 31, 57, 63, 64
St. Hyacinth Church 40, 60, 84, 88
St. Joachim Home 69
St. Joseph Home 19, 31, 35, 40, 58, 74
St. Joseph, patron 29, 30, 38, 42, 50, 51, 56
St. Louis/East St. Louis, MO 77, 78, 80, 81, 88
St. Stanislaus Kostka College xv, 31, 63
St. Stanislaus Kostka Parish and Rectory viii, xiv, xv, xvii, xviii, xix, 4, 11, 22, 24, 27, 39, 45, 56, 60, 61, 86, 89, 96, 100
St. Stanislaus Kostka School, St. Louis 80
St. Theresa Home 69
St. Vincent Home 60
Sts. Peter and Paul Church 66
Suwalski, Mrs. 90
Swiatkowski, Rev. Luke 89
Swierczek, Rev. S. 84

T

Theophilia, Sr. Mary (Sophie Stasiek) 82
Thiel, Mr. John 38
Third Order of St. Francis xviii, 4, 5, 10, 11, 37, 43, 63, 96
Toriskie, Sr. Jeanne Marie 100, 118-119, 121-124
Tudyka, Rev. 90

V

Veronica, Sr Mary (Louise Maka) 59, 82
Vincent, Sr. Mary (Maryann Czyzewska) 61, 67, 78, 80, 85, 94
Vows 62, 63, 68, 73, 74, 79, 82, 84, 87, 89, 91, 96

W

Welfare Society 22
Whiting, IN 88
Widows 3
Wiedemann, Mr. 46
Wing, Claire M. 114, 125
Wisinski, Mathilda 25–125, 35

Y

Youngstown, OH 88

Z

Zapala, Rev. W., C.R. 82
Zita, Sr. Mary (Frances Kosmala) 80

Made in the USA
Monee, IL
05 January 2021